Driven To Our Knees

Help For Those Struggling Through The Trials Of Life

By Vic Coleman

Driven To Our Knees

Driven To Our Knees
by Vic Coleman

Published by:
Victor Coleman
7544 FM 1960 Road East #1015
Humble, TX 77346

Copyright © 2008 Victor D. Coleman

All rights reserved. No part of the contents of this book may be reproduced or transmitted in any form or by any means without the written permission of Victor D. Coleman.

ISBN 978-0-6151-8883-6

Bible references are from the New International Version (NIV) unless otherwise noted.

Scripture taken from the HOLY BIBLE, NEW INTERNATIONAL VERSION
Copyright © 1973, 1978, 1984 International Bible Society. Used by permission of Zondervan Bible Publishers

Contact Information:
Vic Coleman ♦ 7544 FM 1960 Road East #1015 ♦ Humble, TX ♦ 77346 ♦ viccoleman@yahoo.com
Blog site: VicColeman.com

Driven To Our Knees

Table of Contents

Acknowledgements 4
Introduction 5
Character, Not Circumstance 7
I Thirst: Jesus In the "Valley" 16
Prepared for Service 19
Are You Tired of Manna? 26
This Thing Called Faith: Abram and His Son 32
The Authority of His Word 38
How Do You Get Close To God? 43
God Takes His Time…For Our Good 50
Facing Life's Challenges 55
How To Know The Voice of God 61
God's Word: Can I Live By It? 67
Driven To Our Knees 72
Overcoming Obstacles 78
God is Good 84
Complete Surrender: The Key to Victory 92
Answers To Prayers 99
Your Blessing Book 103

Acknowledgements

I must first acknowledge my Lord and Savior, Jesus Christ, who, out of His goodness has saved my family and me. There is no life without Him. He is my life.

Secondly, I must acknowledge my wife, Virginia. Everyday it becomes more obvious how blessed I am to have her as my wife. I could not imagine being without her.

Thirdly, I'd like to acknowledge our sons, Lionel (LT) and Steve. Both of them have made my life more fulfilling. I've had the pleasure of being a parent and a friend to both.

No one accomplishes anything of any consequence without the help and influence of others along the way. I am very grateful to my mother and all my family and friends.

I am especially grateful to Pastor Carl A. Lucas, Sr., and his wife Evelyn Lucas of God First Church. Together they have been consistent models of how to put God first in our lives.

Driven To Our Knees

Introduction

I have had the pleasure of leading a home-based Bible study for several years now. Most of the lessons have revolved around lessons the Lord was teaching me through the trials and difficult times in my life. As I went through these periods, I began to read my Bible more intensely in search of answers, encouragement, and a closer relationship with God. Typically as I read, a certain passage would catch my attention. I would read it over and over again, take notes, and meditate on the passage. I would also pray and listen to what the Lord was telling me. Next I would begin to write. The result was the next Bible study lesson.

The next time we gathered for our study session, I would jokingly begin by saying, "Well, the Lord was on my case again. Here's the lesson for this evening." As I passed out copies of the study, our host would smile and laughingly say, "Good! Brother Coleman, I like it when He gets on your case."

We would laugh, but the truth of the matter was that the lessons I experienced turned out to be most effective in changing my life and the lives of others. They were written out of pain, anguish, sadness, disappointment, and bewilderment. They were written when I was driven to my knees in search of answers; in search of a "touch" from the Lord.

Although the foundation of these studies was based on some trial I was experiencing, I learned so much about God, His character, and His ways. Through these studies you'll learn about living by God's Word, the authority of Christ, why bad things happen, faith, how God prepares us for service, and how to listen to God among many other concepts and principles. And as with me, as your relationship with Him grows, your response to and perspective of God will change. So as you review these lessons, read the scriptures listed in the lesson, take notes, and discuss with others. You will find something beneficial whether you are "going through" or not. In addition, you will find hope, encouragement, peace, and understanding.

To aide in developing your relationship with the Lord, I strongly recommend that you create your own "testimony book". Several sheets have been provided at the end of the book. Write down your prayer requests and the day the Lord answers the prayer. Also, document the blessings He has given you on a daily basis. Over time you will be able to see more clearly His hand in your life and your own words will be an encouragement to you and others in time of need.

Driven To Our Knees

I wish that everyone will take to heart the words spoken to Joshua when God said, "…I will never leave you nor forsake you…" (Joshua 1:5, NIV) and know that God is with you even through the tough times.

We will all be "driven to our knees" many times in our lives. The key to victory is in how we respond to these trials. As you read these lessons, get out your Bible, follow along, and listen to what the Spirit has to say.

Driven To Our Knees

Character, Not Circumstance

Introduction
Recently I went through a personal crisis where it seemed like my enemies were poised to attack me from all angles. The battlegrounds included work, home, finances, my marriage, my ministries in the church, and my personal goals. Every major area of my life (except for my health) seemed to have a physical and/or spiritual enemy. Feeling surrounded, I followed the advice of my pastor and prayed – hard. What the Lord showed me has changed my life.

This lesson focuses on how we are to place our faith in the character of God and not in our circumstances or how we *imagine* our circumstances should change. This principle is based on four basic aspects of His character – Faithfulness, Love, Authority, and Power.

Scriptures Used In This Lesson
Judges 6 – 8
James 5:16
Philippians 4:7 – 9
Isaiah 55:8 – 13
Colossians 1:19 – 21

Background
The text for this lesson focuses on the life of Gideon (Judges 6 – 8). Important aspects of God's character are revealed in His interaction with Gideon and the deliverance of Israel from their enemies. As we study this lesson we will see how we should never depend on our imagination of how our situation should change. God is so much bigger.

Completely Surrounded
Israel had sinned (again) before the Lord. As a result, they were conquered by the Midianites, the Amalekites, and other nations from the east. So complete was their dominance that the Bible says:

> "They (the Midianites) came up with their livestock and their tents like swarms of locust. It was impossible to count the men and their camels; they invaded the land and ravage it." (Judges 6:5, NIV)

This scripture reminded me of how sometimes our problems can seem to surround us and attack us from every angle. We feel overwhelmed. It can be one big problem or many "smaller" problems. The Bible also says that,

Driven To Our Knees

> *"Midian so impoverished the Israelites that they cried out to the Lord for help" (verse 6, NIV)*

The threatening advance of the Midianites caused the Israelites to cry out to the Lord (v. 7).

There may be times in your life when you feel so powerless and conquered that all you can do is call out to the Lord. If we're not careful, your concern over our circumstances will turn into worry; worry will turn to despair; despair will lead to fear, and fear can lead to a separation from God (so sin). Thinking about this scenario, where is the battle taking place? The battlefield is in the *mind*. The scriptures say, "For as he thinketh in his heart, so is he" (Proverbs 23:7, KJV). So as we think "bad" thoughts, our emotions become entangled with the mental picture that has developed in our minds. Our emotions act as ropes that pull us down the slippery slope of despair. If we think and feel we are defeated, we will certainly act defeated, or find a way to make defeat come to pass.

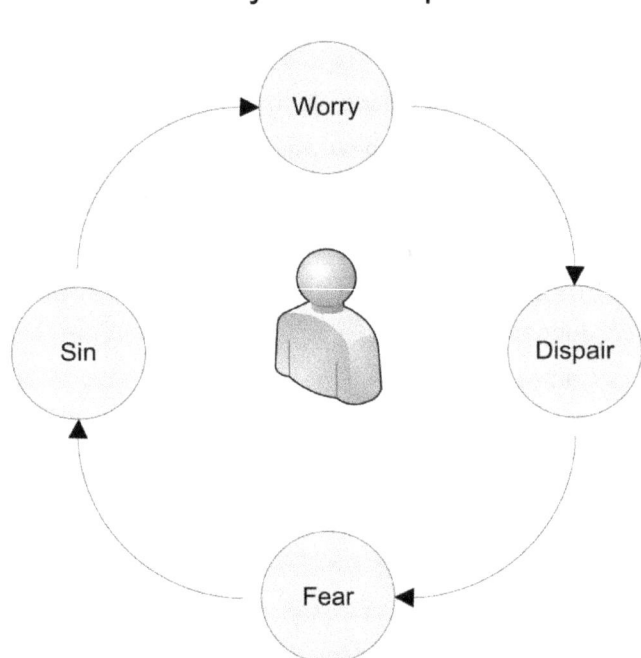
The Cycle of Dispair

It is so important during these times that we keep our focus on God's Word and not our circumstances. It is at these times that we can be the most open to the Lord. Times of adversity can drive us closer to the Lord than times of ease, comfort and pleasure. That is why He sometimes allows us to go through adversity...to drive us towards Him.

Adversity does the following:

- It humbles us.
- It forces us to seek Him (usually after we have exhausted all other options).
- It forces us to put Him first in our prayer life. We tend to pray more intently, with fewer mental distractions.
- It focuses our thoughts on Him and Him alone.
- It helps us to believe in Him more (because we have no other place to go).
- It forces us to be more obedient.
- It forces our prayers to be more sincere, intense and heartfelt. (see James 5:16)

Driven To Our Knees

It is possible to get to this state without adversity, but given our human nature and natural tendencies, we routinely miss the mark. So God allows adversity to come our way.

Can you think of a time when you or someone you know responded to adversity "inappropriately"? Can you think of a time when you or someone responded properly to adversity? What happened to him or her? How did their situation ultimately turn out?

An Expression of His Love and Faithfulness

In Judges 6: 7 – 14, we can see an expression of God's love and faithfulness towards Israel. We are told that Israel had sinned against God in verse 1. This was certainly not the first time they had done so. In verse 10 we are told that Israel did not listen to God. But in verse 14, we see God calling Gideon to save the people from their enemies. I found this response of the Lord interesting. Here's why.

God had a sinful people with whom he had contended ever since they left Egypt under the guidance of Moses. They engaged in disbelief, disobedience, the worship of other gods, and many other acts, attitudes, and words that separated them from Him. They wandered in the desert forty years, were led to the Promised Land and afterwards, continued the pattern of sin. This is how the Midianites came to invade and conquer the land in verse 1.

You would think that after hundreds of years of these cycles of sin, God would have completely destroyed the nation and started over with some other nation. But he didn't. He kept Israel from being completely destroyed. He always spared a remnant so that the nation would survive. Why? Did He enjoy this cycle of sin?

Why do you think God tolerates our cycle of sin? Why do parents tolerate "cycles of sin" from their children? What expectations do parents have of their children? Do they expect them to be perfect?

Let's try to look at it from His perspective. We try to instruct our children in proper behavior patterns from an early age. As little children, they miss the mark repeatedly. Sometimes they will do and say things which break our hearts. When they do, do we kill our children and start a new family? No, we correct them as often as they need and continue to work with them. Why – because we love them.

Driven To Our Knees

Our children are part of us; they share our DNA. Our heartfelt desire is for them to prosper and do well in life. Our love is measured by the giving of our time, money, attention, affection, and the supply of their needs and wants. Our faithfulness is measured by the continuation of our expressions of love through out their lives. This is what God was exhibiting in verses 7 – 14 towards Israel; not final judgment and punishment, but faithfulness and love.

God loves us; we are a part of Him; we share His "DNA" (the Holy Spirit). We can never be separated from His love. His heartfelt desire is for us to prosper and do well in life, and to have a deep and abiding relationship with Him. His love is measured by His giving (life, family, jobs, hobbies, talents, peace of mind, health, etc.). His faithfulness is measured by the continual expression of love towards us throughout our lives. Faithfulness and Love are two aspects of God's character upon which you can always rely.

Authority – What Does It Mean?
When we say that someone has authority over something or someone else, many images come to mind.

What does "authority" mean? Give some examples.

"Authority" used in this passage, comes from the Greek word "exousia" which means:

1. power of choice, liberty of doing as one pleases
2. physical and mental power
    a. the ability or strength with which one is endued, which he either possesses or exercises
3. *the power of influence* and of right (privilege)
4. a convincing force
5. the power of rule or government (the power of him whose will and commands must be submitted to by others and obeyed)

Authority - Verses 36 – 40
Verses 36 – 40 of Judges 6, is a simple but powerful example of the authority of God. If we read the verses superficially, we may conclude that God performed a "small" miracle. But there is much more in these verses. God demonstrated His authority over the physical laws that govern our world. In light of the definitions above, God exercised His *power of influence* to manipulate the dew in a manner that benefited Gideon.

Driven To Our Knees

God created nature. He is not bound by the laws He created. He has authority over our physical world. With that said, is there anything in our lives that God cannot change? No. He has authority over every aspect of our lives.

Can you think of some times when God saved you or someone else from a car wreck, or kept you from being killed or sick?

More Love and Faithfulness

These verses also show God expressing acts of love and faithfulness towards Gideon. In verse 36, Gideon questions what God had already told him. He was fearful and doubted God. Gideon had been given a sign from God in verses 17 – 22. God could have responded to this disbelief by punishing Gideon.

How would you feel if your children doubted your word? How do you think God feels when we doubt Him?

Fortunately God is not like us. He complied with Gideon's request. This was another act of love, faithfulness and mercy.

Power, Power, and More Power

God has all power. Power is:

- ability to act or produce an effect
- possession of control, authority, or influence over others

In Judges 7:1 – 8, God had reduced the number of Gideon's army from 32,000 to 300 men. Verses 2 – 3 provide the reasoning: so that the nation of Israel would not boast that they defeated their enemies; God would get the glory.

God, sensitive to Gideon's "concerns" over defeating 120,000 men with 300, demonstrates His "influence over others" (power) in Judges 7:9 – 16. God caused Gideon to sneak down to the right tent, at the right time, just as one man was telling another about a dream he had. Just as Gideon arrived, he overhears the man not only mentioning Gideon's name, but the name of Gideon's father. There was no mistake of whom they were speaking. The men also mentioned God by name, and mentioned what God had already told Gideon. Coincidence, or God's "control and influence over others"?

Driven To Our Knees

Obviously, God's power is demonstrated in these verses. In verses 7:19 – 25, we see how God's power defeated Israel's enemies.

Character Not Circumstance

Gideon had no idea how God was going to defeat an army of 120,000 men. He could not have imagined that he would not have to lift a sword. He could not have imagined that all he had to do was hold a lamp and shout with 300 men.

In the same manner, we have no idea how God will work the victory in our lives over the trials and tribulations. We can't imagine what He will do in the future. If we begin to trust in our imaginations, i.e., how we imagine we would like for Him to work, we will end up frustrated and disappointed. God is bigger than our imaginations. Read Isaiah 55:8 – 13.

> *"For my thoughts are not your thoughts, neither are your ways my ways," declares the LORD. "As the heavens are higher than the earth, so are my ways higher than your ways and my thoughts than your thoughts.*
>
> *As the rain and the snow come down from heaven, and do not return to it without watering the earth and making it bud and flourish, so that it yields seed for the sower and bread for the eater, so is my word that goes out from my mouth: It will not return to me empty, but will accomplish what I desire and achieve the purpose for which I sent it. You will go out in joy and be led forth in peace; the mountains and hills will burst into song before you, and all the trees of the field will clap their hands. Instead of the thornbush will grow the pine tree, and instead of briers the myrtle will grow. This will be for the LORD's renown, for an everlasting sign, which will not be destroyed." (NIV)*

If God always worked according to how we would like for Him, based on our imaginations, we would begin to trust in our minds and not Him. We would miss experiencing Him, His power and glory.

> *What would trusting in ourselves do to our relationship with Him?*

God didn't send His Son to die for nothing. Jesus died to restore the relationship between God and man. Read Colossians 1:19 – 21. God hates anything that would damage that relationship.

> *For God was pleased to have all his fullness dwell in him (Christ), and through him to reconcile to himself all things, whether things on earth or things in heaven, by making*

peace through his blood, shed on the cross. Once you were alienated from God and were enemies in your minds because of [a] your evil behavior. (NIV)

What Is The Object Of Your Faith?

So what can we put our trust in? The *character* of God. There were four aspects of God's character demonstrated in Gideon's life upon which we can *always* rely. To help you remember, I've created an acronym, F. L. A. P.

You can trust in God's:

- *F*aithfulness
- *L*ove
- *A*uthority
- *P*ower

Circumstances change; people change; your perspective on life changes over time. God doesn't change; He is immutable. He is the only one upon which we can rely.

Our spouses or parents may love us, but they are flawed. They are not as faithful as we need them to be, nor do they have all authority and power. They may have good intension, but lack the *F*, *A*, and *P* that we need in desperate times. Only God can supply the full *FLAP* that we need. Our confidence in Him will be the key to having "peace of mind" in a stormy situation.

Driven To Our Knees

Summary

Focusing on the character of God, i.e., His Faithfulness, Love, Authority, and Power, gave me comfort and peace during my stormy period – a time when I felt surrounded and out of control. I had imagined how God could deliver me, but became more frustrated because my circumstances were not turning out as I had thought. I had a complete "movie" in my mind of how God would/should work. None of it came to pass. Now I see that it would have damaged our relationship; I would not have learned to truly trust Him.

I've trusted God before, but He is taking that trust to a new level. In a sense, He won't allow me to stay in first grade; I *will* move on to second grade, no matter how comfortable I am in first grade. As time goes on, I am seeing God work in ways I couldn't have imagined. Gradually I am letting go of my imagination and focusing more on His character. As I do, I see the working of miracles.

I don't like what I'm going through, but I know that relationship is what He wants, and demands. He will not accept superficiality from me; He demands intimacy. And intimacy begins with trusting in His character not circumstance.

How close are you to God?

Driven To Our Knees

Notes:

Driven To Our Knees

I Thirst: Jesus In the "Valley"

Scriptures Used In This Lesson
John 19:28 – 30
Psalm 22
Psalm 23

As we read the above passage in John 19, we see that this was Jesus' "valley" experience, i.e., He was in the valley of the shadow of death. These verses also say the "Scriptures would be fulfilled". What Scriptures were they talking about?

Prophetic scriptures about Jesus can be found in the books like Amos, Psalms, Zachariah and Isaiah. The one we'll focus on is Psalm 22. If you want to get an idea of what Jesus may have been feeling and thinking while on the cross, read Psalm 22. There are several key verses that illustrate that Jesus was in the "Valley". Verse 1 of Psalm 22 says:

> *"My God, My God, why have you forsaken me?"* This is quoted verbatim by Jesus in Matthew 27: 46.

Verses 7 – 8 speak of men mocking Jesus as he hangs on the cross. This was fulfilled in Matthew 27:43.

Verse 15 speaks of Jesus' tongue sticking to the roof of his mouth. In John 19:28, Jesus says, "I thirst". Verse 18 of Psalm 22 speaks of Jesus' enemies taking his garments and casting lots for his clothing. This was fulfilled in Matthew 27:35.

Going back a little, verse 16 speaks of Jesus being crucified. The amazing thing about this verse is that crucifixion had not been invented when it was written. The Persians invented crucifixion about 500 years after David wrote this Psalm. The Romans, who crucified Christ, didn't officially use crucifixion until about 400 years after the Persians. So this verse is truly prophetic; David wrote about how Christ would die before crucifixion had been invented, and about 1000 years before Christ was born.

So how does all this relate to your daily life? If God has told you anything or given you a promise, then it will come to pass. Whether it's been a day since He's spoken to you or a decade, He will bring it to pass. David wrote this Psalm, under the guidance of the Holy Spirit, 1000 years before the scriptures were fulfilled. And it came to pass…every detail. God is true to His Word.

Driven To Our Knees

Also, notice how Psalm 22, which paints a picture of great suffering, is next to the Psalm the offers great hope...Psalm 23.

The cross was Jesus' "valley" experience. He walked through the valley of the shadow of death. But He was able to look beyond the "valley" towards the "hope" of the Good Shepard (Psalm 23).

When we go through "valley" experiences in our lives, we need to look forward to the same hope that Jesus did...our Good Shepherd.

According to Psalm 23:

- He is a shepherd – a protector
- We will not be in want – He supplies or needs
- He gives us peace and restores us
- He guides us
- He is present with us
- He comforts us
- He will bless abundantly in the midst of our enemies
- He gives us His Spirit which purifies us and makes us Holy
- He provides good things to us
- He loves us every day of our lives
- He allows us to dwell with Him forever

God is truly Good. Our Good God shows us that right beyond our valley experience is hope. So if you *thirst*, know that there are *still waters* coming. Our Heavenly Father will lead us towards them as we fix our eyes upon Him.

Driven To Our Knees

Notes:

Prepared for Service

Introduction

Before we were born, the Lord had a plan for us. Fulfillment of His plans is the key to a rewarding, blessed and fulfilled life. But like an athlete preparing for a major contest, we have to go through training. We can't just "take the field" and start the game. We have to be prepared for service. And like all athletes, sometimes the training is long, hard, and a test of our courage. But if we persevere to the end, we will receive great reward.

Scriptures Used In This Lesson

Jeremiah 29:11 – 13
Isaiah 49:1 – 3
Jeremiah 1:4 – 5
Romans 8:28 – 30
Genesis 41:41 – 46
Genesis 45:7 – 8
Luke 1:27

Background

Recently I have been seeking the Lord concerning a certain trial I have been experiencing. What concerned me was that it seemed as though it was going on, and on, and on, over a number of years. I sought the Lord in prayer, and I couldn't see what I was doing wrong, i.e., there was no discernable sin to which I could point and say, "That's it. That's why I'm going through all this." If I could find something, I would immediately repent to end the trial. I corrected everything I knew to correct, but the trial continued.

What was odd was the fact that during this time, the Lord blessed me in a number of ways. I even started a "blessing book" or journal to document all that He had done for me. As He answered a prayer or provided for a need, I would write it down. After a number of years, I ended up with several notebooks of "blessings". So I was confused. It seemed like I was being punished and blessed at the same time. It didn't make sense. So something else is going on. What was it? I was being prepared for service.

God Has A Plan

God has a plan for your life. There are many scriptures that point to this truth. Jeremiah 29:11 – 13 says:

Driven To Our Knees

> *For I know the plans I have for you," declares the LORD, "plans to prosper you and not to harm you, plans to give you hope and a future. Then you will call upon me and come and pray to me, and I will listen to you. You will seek me and find me when you seek me with all your heart. (NIV)*

Isaiah speaks about the Lord calling him in Isaiah 49:1 – 3:

> *Listen to me, you islands; hear this, you distant nations: Before I was born the LORD called me; from my birth he has made mention of my name. He made my mouth like a sharpened sword, in the shadow of his hand he hid me; he made me into a polished arrow and concealed me in his quiver. (NIV)*

The Lord, speaking of Jeremiah, says in Jeremiah 1:4 – 5:

> *The word of the LORD came to me, saying, "Before I formed you in the womb I knew you, before you were born I set you apart; I appointed you as a prophet to the nations." (NIV)*

And finally in this familiar passage in Romans, we see again that God does have a plan for our lives.

> *And we know that in all things God works for the good of those who love him, who have been called according to his purpose. For those God foreknew he also predestined to be conformed to the likeness of his Son, that he might be the firstborn among many brothers. And those he predestined, he also called; those he called, he also justified; those he justified, he also glorified. (Romans 8:28 – 30, NIV)*

God's specific plan for our lives can take on many "flavors", i.e., it can vary throughout our lives. God's plan for Moses started early in his life with his adoption by Pharaoh's daughter. He then lived under Pharaoh as a son for forty years, learning the mechanics of how to lead. The next season of his life involved being humbled by God for forty years in the desert tending sheep. (A humble spirit is important in being used by God). The final season of Moses' life involved leading the Hebrews out of captivity and through the wilderness for another forty years. Each season of Moses' life was in preparation for his ultimate service…to lead God's people during their wilderness journey, to prepare the next generation to enter the Promised Land, and to learn the ways of God.

Did Moses know or understand God's plan before time? No. God gave Moses enough information to go to the next step (this is important for us to remember). All Moses had to do was trust and obey. Did Moses have to do anything special on his own to prepare for the next step? No. When a new

Driven To Our Knees

season started, God had already prepared him. The previous events of his life prepared him for the next phase. All Moses had to do was trust God and be obedient to God when He called. God did the rest. What Moses couldn't do, God did.

Key Point: God has a plan for our lives. He may not reveal it in its entirety at one time. We have to trust and obey Him to see it fulfilled.

Key Point: God's plan for our lives may be divided into stages, where one stages prepares us for the next.

Key Point: The key to successfully completing each stage of the His plan is to trust and obey Him.

> Can you see God working out a plan in your life? What about the life of someone you know? Maybe you can help someone see God's hand by helping them view things from a different perspective.
>
> What is God's plan for your life? What stage are you in?

Fulfillment Takes Time

God's plan for our lives takes time; sometimes days; sometimes years. Abraham was 75 years old when God told him that he would father a son. So part of God's plan for Abraham's life was to "birth" a new nation. Isaac, the fulfillment of that promise, was born 25 years later.

Again, God chose Moses to lead the nation of Israel out of Egypt, before he was born. God allowed him to grow up in the protected house of Pharaoh for 40 years. It was 40 years later before Moses fulfilled God's ultimate plan for his life.

All of us have a divine plan for our lives, but sometimes it takes years before its final fulfillment. When we are in the midst of a storm that seems to last a long time, we need to take a long-term view and ask these questions:

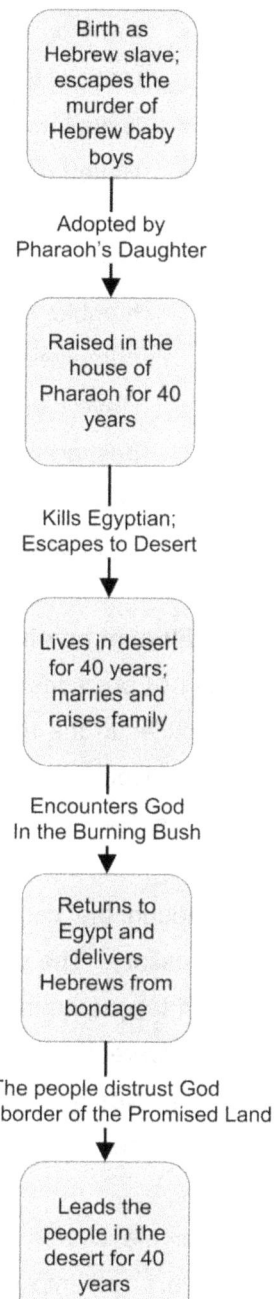

Driven To Our Knees

- Is there any known sin that I intentionally and defiantly hold on to or keep committing? If so, repent immediately.
- Am I responding to the storm the way I should, i.e., in a manner that shows trust and obedience to God?
- Am I on course to emerge from the storm stronger than when I entered? (my wife and I realized that our marriage is stronger due to the storms we have endured)
- Have I used this storm as an opportunity to develop a closer relationship with the Lord?
- Have I asked God to give me the long-term view during this trial or have I been too focused on the present pain?
- Have I sincerely asked God to receive glory from this trial? (this questions helps us to have a humble, selfless attitude during the storm; this question places the focus on Him and not on ourselves)
- Have I sincerely asked God to show me what I am to learn during this trial? (ask not out of desperation, but a sincere desire to be more like Christ)
- Have I kept my eyes on the Lord, or have I been consumed by the storm? (don't look at the bigness of the storm, but the bigness of our God)

Fulfillment Involves Pain

Both of our sons played high school football. Practice would begin in early August with two-a-day practices in the hot summer sun. I would get hot just watching them practice, so you can imagine how uncomfortable it was for them. Each practice would end with some sort of conditioning - wind sprints, "bear crawls", or some other activity that would test their stamina *after* a two-hour practice.

Although the conditioning after practice was the least favorite part of practice, it was the most necessary. The purpose of the conditioning was to increase their endurance so they would not faint from fatigue during critical parts of the game; you did not want your players losing a game because they were too tired. Also, the conditioning developed "mental toughness"; players had to push themselves mentally to complete the conditioning drill. Although they were hot and tired, they had to determine in their minds that they would push on and complete the drill to the best of their abilities.

Over the course of a season, the conditioning drills became less of a requirement because the players "got into shape" physically and mentally. By October, they could run the same drills after practice with ease; they were better equipped to execute the coaches' plays during game; they had a better chance to win.

Being prepared for God's service sometimes involves the "pain of conditioning", i.e., we go through seemingly long periods of distress, discomfort, and pain. If we quit in the midst of the "drill", we will

Driven To Our Knees

not be in condition to "win the game", i.e., do the work God has called us to do. Fulfilling God's plan will give us more joy, satisfaction, and reward than we could ever imagine. But none of that will come to pass if we grow weary and faint.

Just as an athlete running his tenth 40-yard sprint after practice, we must keep our eyes on the goal, which is, "This is getting me ready to be successful in the work God has called me to do." This has to be our mindset through the storm.

The book of Genesis tells the story of Joseph, Jacob's (Israel's) son. In chapter 37, we discover that his brothers hated him and sold him into slavery. This was the beginning of Joseph's "conditioning drill". Soon after spending time in Potiphar's house, Joseph was put in charge of managing the household. Then he was falsely accused of trying to rape Potiphar's wife. As a result, he was thrown into prison. After a short time, Joseph was put in charge of running the prison. After a number years, he was suddenly, and miraculously released and was put in charge of managing the affairs of the entire nation (Genesis 41:41 - 46). He was second only to Pharaoh.

Joseph spent about 13 years in his "conditioning" stage. It was not pleasant; there were times that were physically and emotionally painful. But during it all, he kept his eyes on the Lord. His "reward" came all of a sudden and was greater than he could imagine.

In Genesis 45:7 – 8, Joseph reveals God's ultimate plan. God used the slavery and prison to develop Joseph's management skills. God placed Joseph in the position of running Egypt, so at the right time, he would be in a position to save the tiny nation of Israel (his family) from starvation. Only God could have come up with such an elaborate plan.

Joseph did not faint in his faith. He was faithful through the stormy period in his life, through the "conditioning drills".

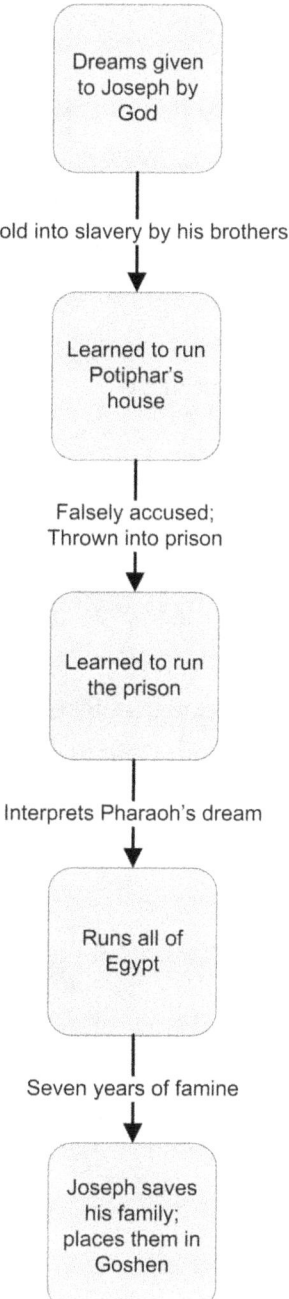

Fulfillment Ends In Reward

As with Joseph, the fulfillment of God's plan reaps rewards for us and those close to us. Joseph was able to save his entire family. Moses was able to save an entire nation (2 to 4 million people). Jesus was able to save an entire race.

The key to surviving the long "conditioning drills" is to focus on God, use the time to get in right relationship with him, to have faith, and obey His commands. (Remember that the object of our faith is in the character of God, not a series of events that will give us relief). **Because of God's goodness, He will reward us.** Don't be surprised if the reward comes all of a sudden and is greater than you had imagined.

Summary

As I wrote this study, I reflected on my own life and it helped me keep things in the right perspective. I realize to a greater degree that God *is* in control. It's not my battle; it's His. As my level of faith in Him increases, my stress and distress decreases. That's been a true test for me; if I'm stressed out, I'm not trusting God; I am not behaving like the creator of the universe has enough power to supply my needs. That attitude dishonors God. That is something I don't want to do.

Ask yourself the questions listed under *Fulfillment Takes Time* and be honest with God and yourself. Realize that the quicker we "get into shape", the less necessary are the "conditioning drills".

Driven To Our Knees

Notes:

Driven To Our Knees

Are You Tired of Manna?

Introduction

There was a time in my life where I had a serious need from the Lord. The clock was ticking, the need remained unmet, I prayed to God, and nothing changed. Then I thought, "Don't seem like God is going to answer this prayer. I got to do things on my own. Seems like He just led me to where I am today and just left me. I'll just take care of myself." I knew God had done a lot for me, but I needed Him to work a certain way right now. I followed Him before, but where was He now?

This lesson is a study of certain events in the history of Israel after Moses led them out of Egypt, the Exodus. Their responses to their crises can teach us the appropriate way to respond to the crises in our lives and how God views our "typical" response. Getting totally consumed by the situation at hand can cause us to miss some of God's greatest blessings in our lives.

Scriptures Used In This Lesson

Exodus 15:22 – 25
Exodus 16:1 – 5
Exodus 16:11 – 15, 16 – 30, 30 – 35
Exodus 17:1 – 3
Numbers 14

Background

Moses had just led the fledgling nation of Israel out of Egyptian slavery with a great deliverance. Over the previous days, they had witnessed the mighty hand of God with locust, gnats, water turning to blood, and the death angel killing the first born of those whose homes were not covered by the blood of a lamb. They had just witnessed the parting of the Red Sea, where they walked across the sea on dry ground. They had just witnessed the death of the Egyptians who were chasing them. They had witnessed the mighty hand of God in numerous ways. And now they meet their first crisis as a free people.

They were Thirsty - Exodus 15:22 – 25

The Israelites had traveled three days after crossing the Red Sea and they became thirsty. When they came to Marah, they "grumbled" against Moses. The need was real – water for about 3 million people – men, women and children. But their grumbling was more like the response of a people who had *never* seen the miracles of God, as opposed to someone who had just experienced a miracle three days earlier. God moved (again) and 3 million people had water to drink.

Driven To Our Knees

Hunger in the Desert - Exodus 16:1 – 5

The second crisis comes when the people became hungry. Notice how they grumbled against Moses and Aaron again.

Verse 3 is very revealing. It tells of the mindset of the people, i.e., how they were thinking. They had preferred to be back in Egypt, as slaves, where they thought they would have plenty to eat. It was only a month before where they were praying to the Lord to deliver them from Egyptian slavery.

God Provides Again - Exodus 16:11 – 15, 16 – 30, 31 – 35

Again, God provided for the need. Not only did He provide quail, He provided manna. Manna comes from a word that means, "What is it?" When the Israelites first saw the manna, they did not know what it was. So that became the name of this daily provision from God.

Verses 16 – 30 tell how God instructed the people to get as much as manna as they needed (not as much as they wanted). If they gathered more than they were supposed to, the manna turned into maggots. The manna was supposed to provide for their daily needs, i.e., what was necessary to sustain them.

Verses 31 – 35 provide a description of the "bread from heaven" and how it sustained them for 40 years. (Note: an omer is about 2 quarts or ½ gallon).

To get a feel for the size of this miracle, let's do some math. First, let's assume that an omer of manna weighed about a pound (we don't know for sure, but we need a starting point). So, each person ate about a pound of manna a day. To feed the nation of Israel required 3 million pounds a day, or 1,500 tons a day. To feed the people for a year, God provided 1,095,000,000 pounds of manna, or 5,475,000 tons/yr. That's a lot of food. And He did it for 40 years.

Key Point: The Manna was to provide for their daily needs, not wants. It was meant to sustain them until they reached the Promised Land.

> *What's the difference between a need and a want? Should God provide all your wants? Why or Why not? Should a parent provide all the wants of a child? Why or Why not?*

***Mishandling* The Next Crisis - Exodus 17:1 – 3**

Now after witnessing the miraculous appearance of 3 million pounds of food each day, what did Israel do at the next crisis? Exodus 17:1 – 3 tells us that they complained.

Why did Israel complain? What are your daily blessings? Which ones do you think

The Decline of Israel

Grumbling → Disbelief → Disrespect towards God → Loss of Fellowship → Sin → Death

40 Years In The Desert

you miss or don't readily recognize? Why don't we recognize God's daily blessings? How can we change that?

Grumbling Against The Father - Numbers 14
Continually grumbling against God can have some very serious consequences in our lives. When we constantly complain about what we don't have, it develops a mindset, i.e., a way of thinking that can lead us away from God. Here's how?

Constant or habitual grumbling → Disbelief
Disbelief → Disrespect for God
Disrespect for God → Loss of Fellowship with God
Loss of Fellowship with God → Sin
The Wages of Sin → Death

The 14th chapter of Numbers is very revealing. Moses had sent out 12 men into the Promised Land to spy the region. After 40 days the spies came back with their report. The group reported that the land was "flowing with milk and honey", meaning that it was very fruitful and fertile, like God told them. But 10 of the men saw only the bigness of the enemies in the land and the obstacles they would have to conquer. They spread fear among the people. The people became so fearful that the people wanted to kill Moses and Aaron and to go back to Egypt.

Driven To Our Knees

Key Point: Rebelling against God's anointed messengers, His instructions, or provisions, is like rebelling against God Himself.

Israel threatened Moses and Aaron directly, but God took it personally. Read Numbers 14:10 – 11. Notice the Lord asked, "How long will these people treat *me* with contempt?" What was behind the grumbling – a lack of faith in God's ability to handle the situation.

Here is what Israel had witnessed in the previous months:

- Thousands or even millions of first born being slain by the death angel if they were not covered by the blood of a lamb
- Leaving Egypt with riches given to them by the Egyptians (Exodus 12:35 – 36)
- The parting of the Red Sea and walking through the sea on dry ground (Exodus 12:21 – 22)
- The slaying of the Egyptians who were chasing them (Exodus 14:26 – 28)
- God appearing physically before them in a pillar of cloud by day, and a pillar of fire by night (Exodus 13:20 – 22)
- Million pounds of food appearing every morning (Exodus 16:11 – 15)

After all this and more, the Israelites grumbled and did not trust God in the midst of every crisis. God took it personally.

> *Over the past year, can you recount the things you know God did for you? Name some. Why do you doubt in the midst of your current crisis?*

Key Point: The pillars of fire and cloud never left Israel. In the same way, the Holy Spirit will never leave you.

So how can you keep from insulting God?

1. Remind yourself of what God has done for you. Keep a diary. Update it daily.
2. Fill your mind with God's Word. Daily reading keeps our "heavenly phone" plugged in. We become more receptive to hear Him, through His Word, other people, prayer, and our circumstances.
3. Confess any hidden sins. We need to have a clean heart and mind when we approach the Lord. We don't need anything hindering our communication with Him.
4. Know that He is sovereign over every aspect of our lives. He has the ability to change anything, at any time, in any way.

5. At the first sign of trouble, pray. Pray in the same manner as Jehoshaphat (2 Chronicles 20:6 – 12)
6. Patiently wait for God's answer. There may be some practical things you can do, like updating your resume if you need a job. But seek clear direction from the Lord and wait patiently for His answer.
7. Be obedient. Once you receive directions from God, do it. Even if it doesn't make sense at the time. Obedience is better than sacrifice (I Samuel 15:22).
8. Always, in good times and bad, give God praise for *Who* He is. His very nature deserves our praise.

Summary

Getting tired of manna is the result of not recognizing the value of what God gives us on a daily basis. Yes, we have needs, serious ones, but we should, in praise, go to the One who will supply all your needs. God takes lack of faith personally. It's an assault on His character. Let's not insult the One who loves us most and spend "40 years in the desert" needlessly.

Driven To Our Knees

Notes:

Driven To Our Knees

This Thing Called Faith: Abram and His Son

Introduction

Lately I've been going through a series of trails...one right after another. Some of them have been fairly intense. During the day, my focus fades between my circumstances and scriptures I memorized from the Word. Even though I read the Bible routinely, I decided to search my Bible to look for comfort and specific answers to what was going on in my life. My search was like walking down a winding, dry, rocky path towards a water well called "Faith". What is this thing called "Faith"? To get a better understanding, we'll take a look at the life of Abram and his son.

Background

Abram, later to be renamed Abraham by God, lived about 2100 BC in the land of Ur in Mesopotamia. Mesopotamia comes from a Greek word meaning "between the rivers". Those rivers are the Tigris and the Euphrates, which run through modern Iraq.

One day God told Abram to leave this land and "go to the land I will show you." (Gen. 12:1 NIV). He also told him that he would be "the father of many nations." We're all familiar with this story, but as I walked down my winding road, I took a closer look at his life, compared it to mine, and thought about the promises God made to him; I imagined how Abram must have felt. I then wondered, "How did Abram believe God?"

Scriptures for This Lesson

Genesis 12:1 – 5
Genesis 15:1 – 6
Hebrews 11:11 – 12
Genesis 16
Hebrews 11:17 – 19
Genesis 22

God Said, "Go!", So He Went

In Genesis 12:1, we are told that God spoke to Abram and commanded him to:

> "Leave your country, your people and your father's household and go to the land I will show you."

In verses 2 – 3 God makes a promise to Abram. The first part of verse 4 was really the verse that made me stop and think:

Driven To Our Knees

> *"So Abram left, as the Lord had told him;"*

For all this to take place, several things had to happen:

1. Abram had to hear God's voice and know that it was He Who was speaking
2. Abram had to trust God's intentions for him
3. Abram had to obey

The tradition of the culture at that time was that a family stayed together. The sons inherited their father's land and wealth, and raised their own families on the same land. For Abram to leave, without a full explanation from God, was a big step of faith. The obstacles Abram faced were:

1. He did not know where he was going and could not rationally explain his leaving to others
2. His family may have interpreted his actions as rebellion, foolishness or insulting
3. He had to be sure that God was talking to him and it wasn't his own imagination

In spite of all this, Abram obeyed God and left his home.

Key Point: There are times in the life of a child of God where we are instructed to do things which on the surface don't make sense, are viewed as foolish or crazy, or may cause others to feel hurt or insulted for a time. The key is *knowing* the voice of God and obeying.

> *Has God ever instructed you to do something that seemed to be "crazy"? How did you respond? How did others respond at first? After time had passed? How did you know it was God? Did you know immediately or find out sometime later?*

Key Point: It's wise to seek the Lord first for permission before telling others what He's told you. Sometimes keeping God's word to yourself makes obedience much easier.

A Paradox

In Chapter 15, God speaks to Abram in a vision. It is clear that Abram knew the voice of God. God comforts him and tells him that He is his "shield" and "very great reward".

> *What do you think God meant by saying that He was Abram's "shield" and "very great reward"? Does the same apply to us today? Why or why not?*

In verse 2, Abram asks God, "What can you give me since I remain childless?" Abram was already a very wealthy man (Gen. 13:1 – 2). Having children was the only thing he lacked. But having offspring to pass on the family's name, possessions, and traditions was very important in Abram's culture. A woman's status in society could be measured by whether or not she had children. A man with many sons was admired. Childless couples were pitied and viewed as not having God's favor.

Abram lived a life that was a paradox. On the one hand, he was exceedingly rich. But on the other hand, he was poor. He knew God had led him, protected him and blessed him exceedingly. Yet, he lacked one great blessing in life. A blessing that even "godless" people enjoyed…a son. Now God was promising Abram a son, but Abram was 75 years old.

During my trials, I could see God's blessings in my life. He had brought me through many situations with a "miracle", i.e., something happened where I could not deny that I had been "delivered" by the hand of God. But I was still in the midst of a severe trial. There were times where I didn't know how to respond.

Abram responded appropriately. Verse 15:6 is the key. Against "common sense" and what seemed natural, Abram believed God.

Key Point: In the midst our paradoxes, where we are experiencing a trial, but we can see "the hand of God", we must believe in God's faithfulness.

Key Point: In the midst of our paradoxes, we need to view the "hand of God" as assurance and encouragement that He is with us and will not leave us. We should focus on His promise to be our "shield" and "exceeding great reward", and not on the circumstances.

> *Why is it so hard for us to believe God? What are some obstacles to believing Him? How can we overcome each one of these obstacles?*

Obstacles To Abraham's Blessings

Abraham:
- Did not know where he was going
- Did not have a "rational" explanation for the move
- May have encountered opposition from family members and friends
- Had to be sure that it was God talking to him and not his imagination

Meddlin' In God's Business
Chapter 16 is a classic example of "meddlin' in God's business. Sarai (later renamed by God as Sarah) was logical. She was using "common sense" in convincing her husband to have an offspring by Hagar, an Egyptian servant. She "knew" it was impossible for her to have children because of her age. So if God told her husband that he was to have children, and she was too old, it only made sense that Abram was to have children through someone younger than she.

Driven To Our Knees

She may not have doubted what God had told her husband, but she *assumed* the way God would fulfill His Word. Yes, it made sense. Yes, her intentions were good. But she could not have been more wrong in her assumptions.

Key Point: Doing things based on "good intentions" doesn't mean that you are doing things God's way.

> *Do you know of a situation where you or someone else took a course of action, based on good intentions, but later found out that it was the wrong action to take? Why did it end up being the wrong course of action? Did you/they have all the facts when they made their decision? What role did emotion play in the decision? What role did logic play in the decision?*

Hagar did have Ishmael when Abram was 87 years old. Ishmael did become a great nation as God promised. His descendents are known today as Arabs. Isaac's descendants are known today as Jews. The whole Arab/Israeli conflict started with one well-intentioned, "wrong" act 4100 years ago.

Key Point: Always ask God for guidance, even when the way out seems "obvious".

Key Point: When we meddle in God's business, the consequences can be far reaching.

> *Have you ever meddled in God's business? Are you about to now? Have you asked God first before moving?*

You Want Me To Do What?!
Chapter 22 tells the story of God's ultimate test for Abraham. God instructed Abraham to sacrifice, i.e., kill his son, Isaac. This chapter really got me thinking. How do you balance the love for your child verses being obedient to God? What was going on in Abraham's mind?

Several factors were in play here that shaped Abraham's response:

1. Abraham had had about 40 years of knowing, hearing, and following the voice of God.
2. The fact that Isaac was alive was a testimony to God's faithfulness and power.
3. Abraham was still rich materially. Again, everyday was a testimony of God's faithfulness and power.
4. Abraham thought if God could give a 90 year old woman (Sarah) a son, He could certainly bring Isaac back to life.

Driven To Our Knees

Read Hebrews 11:17 – 19. The key phase is, "By faith". Abraham had such a close relationship with God that he was know as a "friend of God" (James 2:23).

"Friend" comes from the Greek word "philos" which means:

> friend, to be friendly to one, wish him well
> a) a friend
> b) an associate
> c) he who associates familiarly with one, a companion
> d) one of the bridegroom's friends who on his behalf asked the hand of the bride and rendered him various services in closing the marriage and celebrating the nuptials

The Key To Abraham's Blessings

Abraham:
- Recognized the voice of God
- Trusted God
- Obeyed God

How did Abraham know the voice of God? He had built up a relationship with Him over time so that he knew His voice. God and Abraham were close. This is the same type of relationship we should have with God, except *closer!* We are His children, not just friends. We should know our Father's voice just like we know the voice our earthly parent(s).

How close are you to God? Do you know His voice? If not, why not?

Summary

Reading and thinking about Abram and his Son, taught me several things:

1. I need to have a relationship with my Heavenly Father so close that I "know" His voice instantly.
2. I have to be willing and eager to obey.
3. I need to ask God what my next steps should be in my trial, even if the way seems obvious. I don't want to meddle in His business.
4. Sometimes He may ask me to do something that doesn't make sense on the surface; I need to just obey.
5. If I'm in a paradox, I need to view His Hand as confirmation that He is with me.
6. I need to remember that He is my shield and "exceedingly great reward".
7. God is faithful to His promises, no matter what.

Driven To Our Knees

Notes:

Driven To Our Knees

The Authority of His Word

Introduction

One of the attributes of our Lord that is clearly illustrated in the Bible is the authority of Jesus. Understanding His authority is crucial to having a right relationship with Him and to living a victorious life, no matter what trials we face. Equally important is how we respond to His authority.

This lesson introduces the authority of Christ and focuses on the response of those directly affected by that authority. We will then explore how we should respond to Christ and the benefits we receive.

Scriptures Used In This Lesson

Mark 1:14 – 28
John 1:29 - 42

Background

Our lesson focuses on the beginning of Jesus' ministry in Galilee. Galilee was the most northern portion of Palestine which also included Samaria and Judea. The land consisted of a mixture of races and religions. Groups included Jews, Canaanites, Syrians, Phoenicians, Syrians, and Greeks. People of Galilee even spoke with a certain dialect or accent. Jews living in southern Judea considered themselves more "pure" and orthodox in their traditions than those in the north. They generally despised Galileans. But it was in this environment that Jesus decided to begin His ministry and call His first disciples.

> *Can you think of any advantages or disadvantages to Jesus beginning His ministry in such a "mixed" environment?*

Authority – What Does It Mean?

When we say that someone has authority over something or someone else, many images come to mind.

> *What does "authority" mean? Give some examples.*

"Authority" used in this passage, comes from the Greek word "exousia" which means:

1. power of choice, liberty of doing as one pleases
2. physical and mental power
    a. the ability or strength with which one is endued, which he either possesses or exercises
3. the power of influence and of right (privilege)

Driven To Our Knees

4. a convincing force
5. the power of rule or government (the power of him whose will and commands must be submitted to by others and obeyed)

Authority Over Man

Read Mark 1:14 – 20. In this section we see how Jesus begins by preaching the good news of the Gospel. By just reading this passage, it seems as though Jesus, a stranger, commanded Andrew and Simon Peter to follow Him and they did. But Jesus was not unknown to Andrew and his brother. They had heard about Jesus from John the Baptist. Let's read John 1:29 – 42. The "John" referred to in verse 29 is John the Baptist.

We see from the passage that Andrew and Simon Peter were told that Jesus was the Son of God by John the Baptist. In fact, Andrew told Peter that Jesus was the Messiah. To the Jews, the Messiah was their Priest, King, Savior, and anointed by God Almighty Himself. No one could have more "authority" than the Messiah, except God Himself. So in Mark 1:17, Andrew and Simon Peter didn't hear the voice of a stranger call them – they heard the Son of God, the "One promised by God" call them. The authority of the Messiah was enough for them to immediately drop their nets and follow Him.

If the president of the United States came to your job, called you by name and said, "I need you for a very important assignment that concerns this nation. We need to fly to Washington immediately to begin.", would you question him and try to negotiate a more agreeable time? More than likely, no. Most of us would immediately drop what we were doing, fly to Washington, and call home later. Why, because of the recognized authority of who called us. In the same way, Andrew and Simon Peter recognized the Authority calling them.

Read Mark 1:19 – 20. In this selection, we see that James and John are called and we are told that they left their father. We are not told of Zebedee's reaction, but from this we can make some reasonable assumptions.

> *What does it cost to follow Christ? Will others understand? If they don't should you follow Him anyway? Why or why not? Will everyone recognize His authority?*

Remember authority means: *the power of him whose will and commands must be submitted to by others and obeyed.* Our Messiah has that authority. It was recognized by His disciples and caused them to take action. Because they responded appropriately to His authority:

- They were eye witnesses to great miracles.

- They had to opportunity to see, hear and experience His teachings.
- They received the power of the Holy Spirit and drove out demons and healed the sick.
- They went out, in power, and started the Church, of which we are benefactors 2000 years later.

By responding to Christ authority appropriately, what will you gain? What will you lose if you don't? What keeps us from responding appropriately? How can you change things so you can respond appropriately?

Authority Over the Word

In Mark 1:21 – 22, we see that Jesus taught with authority. In those days, scribes rarely taught. They would simply read the Word and quote rabbis. Jesus, the Living Word, the Word in flesh, was the authority. No one could teach the true meaning of the Torah more so than Jesus. Jesus was the "convincing force" behind the teaching of the Word. By definition, he was an authority.

Authority Over Demons

In Mark 1:23 – 26 we see a demonstration of Jesus' authority (i.e., whose will and commands must be submitted to by others and obeyed). Notice that the demon knew who Jesus was. Jesus did not have to identify Himself to the evil spirit. Nor did Jesus have to provide any information about His position in the Kingdom of God. The evil spirit couldn't help but acknowledge that Jesus was "the Holy One of God".

In verse 24, notice the demon's fear when he saw Jesus, that he and other evil spirits would be destroyed.

At Jesus' very words, the spirit stopped talking and left the man. The authority of Jesus was so evident and powerful, that a demon had no choice but to obey. Now, some questions for us:

If Jesus is our savior and has authority over the physical and spiritual world, why do we sometimes walk in fear? Defeat? Discouragement? Loneliness? Sin?

The short answer - we do not respond appropriately to His authority. The shorter answer – we don't trust Him.

Summary

Read Mark 1:27 – 28. From the NIV, verse 27 reads:

The people were all so amazed…

The authority of Jesus is clearly portrayed in our lesson. He has authority over man, the physical world, and the spiritual world. The key to victory in our lives on a daily basis is in our response to His authority. If we ignore it, we lose. If we acknowledge it, we win. Think of little children and their parents – when children respond appropriately to the authority of the parent, they gain favor, blessings, and pleasant expressions of love. When they don't, they suffer the consequences. Our Father has given us the "keys to the Kingdom" in Jesus Christ. If we learn to acknowledge and live under His authority, we too will be "*all so amazed*", not matter what trial we face.

Driven To Our Knees

Notes:

Driven To Our Knees

How Do You Get Close To God?

Introduction

Anyone who has been in or around church for any significant amount of time has heard the phrase, "You need to get close to God". But what does it mean? How do you do it? How do you get close to an invisible, holy, perfect God? Fortunately, God tells us how in His Word and it's fairly straightforward.

I've read Psalm 15 many times in the past. I thought it was "okay", but I never noticed anything really significant about it…until recently. For some reason the scripture "spoke" to me. It almost seemed like an iceberg, where the bulk of the meaning was just below the surface, and the Lord let me see some of what's down there.

When we get "close to God", we are poised to receive many benefits. We can:

1. Hear and know His voice so we can do His will
2. Acquire wisdom
3. Gain strength to overcome obstacles
4. Stand firm in the midst of storms
5. Have peace of mind
6. Receive healing for our minds and bodies
7. Prosper as He wants us to prosper
8. Pray more effectively for ourselves and others
9. Respond to situations as Jesus would respond
10. Know Him better (the most import one in this list)

So how do we get close to God? Well the Bible makes it clear, as a study of this Psalm will reveal.

Scriptures for This Lesson
Psalm 15:1 – 5
Proverbs 23:7
Proverbs 18:21
Proverbs 6:16-19

Driven To Our Knees

Getting Close – What Does It Mean?

Psalm 15:1 poses the questions, "Who may dwell in the sanctuary of the Lord?", and "Who may live on His Holy Hill?" To really understand what the scripture means, i.e., what it means to "get close", we need to first define some terms used in the verse.

In verse 1, the New International Version of the Bible (NIV) uses the word "dwell". The original Hebrew word means to sojourn, or to seek hospitality with, to assemble oneself, to abide, to lodge as if you're on a journey.

"Sanctuary" is also used in the NIV. "Tabernacle" is used in the King James Version (KJV). They come from the Hebrew word "obel" which means covering, dwelling place, home or tent. It refers to His holy dwelling place. (Originally, the presence of the Lord was in a tent that housed the Ark of the Covenant).

Paraphrasing, verse 1 asks, "Who may lodge and seek hospitality in the dwelling place of the Lord? Who can make their home where the Lord lives and get comfortable?" Not only can you get close to God, but also you can make your home and "get comfortable".

I thought about this for a moment and pictured my family driving to Texas to visit my wife's twin brother. He has a nice home out in the country on a couple of acres. He always shows us "southern hospitality". We are the focus of his attention. He makes accommodations just for us and makes us feel welcome and "at home". In the same sense, when we approach the Lord in His dwelling, we can be welcomed. He wants to welcome us into His presence and make us the focus of His attention. We are special to Him.

The second half of verse 1 asks, "Who may live on your holy hill?" The word "live" comes from the word *shakan* which means to settle down, to abide, to reside, to establish. The word carries with it the sense of an extended stay, not a short visit. So to "shakan" on His holy hill means that it is possible to "settle down" and "reside" in the presence of the Lord. Once you get there, you get to stay! Psalm 15:2 begins to tell us how.

How to Get Close – Step 1

To be in the presence of the Lord, your "walk" must be blameless. The word walk comes from the Hebrew word "halak" which means to behave oneself, to exercise or conduct oneself. "Blameless" comes from a word that means integrity, truth, sincerely, without blemish. So Step 1 is to conduct and behave ourselves with integrity.

What does being a man/woman of integrity mean to you? Do you think integrity is getting lost in our society or is it still a virtue held in esteem? Why or Why not?

The next part of verse 2 relates to the first part, "…who does what is righteous…" "Righteous" carries the meaning of what is legally, morally, or naturally right. These two parts of verse 2 deal with how we conduct ourselves…basically being men and women of integrity in our actions.

From the Amplified Version of the Bible, verse 2 reads as follows. (The emphasis is mine):

"He who walks and lives uprightly and blamelessly, who works rightness and justice and *speaks and thinks the truth in his heart.*"

The last half of the verse is interesting. It speaks to what is inside a person. The one who gets close to God speaks and thinks truth in his heart. God looks at the "inner man". He is more interested in our hearts than what we wear or what others see externally. Righteousness needs to be descriptive of our inner thoughts. If we think on "good things", "good things" will come out of our mouths, and influence our actions.

Key Point: What ever you think about, will greatly influence your actions.

What effect will a "steady diet" of pornography have on a young male? What effect will a "steady diet" of violent television shows have on our kids? What effect will a "steady diet" of sexually explicit music and videos have on a young mind? What effect will a "steady diet" of the word of God have on a young mind?

Have some doubts about the Key Point above? Why do companies spend billions of dollars on television commercials every year? After sixty years of commercials, advertisers know that seeing something repeatedly will eventually affect behavior. Their goal is to influence your behavior so that you will be more inclined to buy their products or services.

Psalm 23:7 says:

For as he thinketh in his heart, so is he: Eat and drink, saith he to thee; but his heart is not with thee. (KJV)

Driven To Our Knees

The Bible says that as we draw closer to God, He will draw closer to us when we seek Him with our *whole* heart.

How to Get Close – Step 2

Psalm 15:3 speaks to another area of our conduct…our words. Words are powerful. By the words of God, the world was created. By words, wars have been started and stopped. By words, men have been elected to the most powerful office in the country. By words sport teams have rallied to stage great "come from behind" victories. The scriptures say:

> "The tongue has the power of life and death…" (Proverbs 18:21, NIV)

As a matter of fact, a study of Proverbs will reveal that how influential our words can be. So to get close to God, we must take care in what we say.

Verse 3 says that one who "dwells with the Almighty" does not speak slander. Slander is defined as:

> To defame; to injure by maliciously uttering a false report respecting one; to tarnish or impair the reputation of one by false tales, maliciously told or propagated.
>
> *How often do we propagate a story about someone that we don't know for sure is true (gossip)? How often do we talk about someone knowing that his or her reputation will be injured by what we say? How often do we say things out of anger knowing that our words will hurt someone else?*

Key Point: Once words are spoken, you can no more "take back your words" than you can "un-eat" yesterday's dinner. Be thoughtful of what you say.

There are certain things that the Lord *hates* and slander is one of them (Proverbs 6:16 -19).

The first part of verse 3 says that a person who gets close to God does not wrong his neighbor. Again we see that our actions and words play a key part in our relationship to God.

One definition of reproach is to charge with a fault in severe language. Again it speaks of the tongue and what we say. This part of the verse didn't address whether or not what we say is true; that's beside the point. It's the intent of our hearts that's at issue. To get close to God, our hearts and words must be right before Him.

Driven To Our Knees

How to Get Close – Step 3

Psalm 15:4 introduces a new concept – hating what's evil and loving what's good. The NIV reads:

> "...who despises a vile man but honors those who fear the LORD, who keeps his oath even when it hurts..."

The word "despise" comes from a Hebrew word which means to disesteem something or someone. In order to get close to God, we have to have the same attitude toward sin that He has...He hates sin, i.e., anything that is contrary to his nature and separates us from Him. (That's why He gave us a new nature and we are "born again").

Do you hate that which is evil in the eyes of the Lord, or do you have a tendency to tolerate evil? Name something that is "evil" in the eyes of the Lord that is common in our society. Do you hate it or have a mild dislike for it, knowing intellectually that it's bad?

Key Point: Being "tolerant" of sin allows that sin to grow and take root.

The last half of the verse speaks to integrity again...keeping your word, even when it hurts. By the Word of God, the universe was created. He holds His Word in high esteem. Even His Son is referred to as "The Word". We should hold our words to a higher standard.

How to Get Close – Step 4

Psalm 15:5 touches on another aspect of our character that is near and dear to our hearts...money. From the NIV it reads:

> "...who lends his money without usury and does not accept a bribe against the innocent..."

It speaks of generosity, fairness, selflessness, and integrity. The book of Proverbs is full of scriptures that refer to the "generous man" and his blessings. Why? Because the Lord is generous, fair, selfless, and defines integrity. The bottom line is that He wants us to be like Him.

The Character Traits of One Who Gets Close to God

Blameless Walk
Integrity
No Slander or Gossip
Do No Wrong To Your Neighbor
Hating What is Evil
Generosity

Driven To Our Knees

Summary

Getting close to God is not an impossible feat; it is not a mystery. We must strive to conduct our actions, words, and "meditations of our hearts", in a manner that is like Him. The more we conform ourselves to His image, the closer we will get to Him…automatically. And the benefits of that closeness will begin to flow…automatically. And this passage ends with a powerful promise, (I like to think of it as a statement of fact) – "He who does these things will never be shaken."

Driven To Our Knees

Notes:

Driven To Our Knees

God Takes His Time…For Our Good

Introduction

Sometimes we may be in a situation that is uncomfortable, painful, fearful, or one that makes us weary over time. If we look closely, we can see God working in other areas of our lives, but where is He now…in this situation? Have you ever wondered why God waits so long to move in our behalf?

Well this lesson attempts to explain why the Lord seems to "take His time". During those times when it seems like God is inactive, we must remember that God never leaves us. He is always faithful. God works things out for our good in a timing that's best for us. He knows the details. We don't. We often don't see the big picture. But, He does. Let's look at the life of Joseph.

Scriptures Used In This Lesson

Genesis 37:1 - 4
Genesis 37:12 - 18, 23 - 28
Genesis 39:1 - 5
Genesis 39:7 - 23
Genesis 41:28 - 40, 46
Genesis 45:4 - 7

Joseph Hated By His Brothers - Genesis 37:1 - 4

Joseph is 17 years old. His father routinely showed him favoritism in front of his brothers. This fueled hatred for Joseph among his brothers.

Joseph sold into slavery - Genesis 37:12 - 18, 23 - 28, 36

Initially Joseph's brothers plotted to kill him. Did Joseph do anything wrong? Did he deserve the hatred he received? Notice in verse 25, Joseph's brothers were eating while he was in the well. They lost all respect for him. No sign of guilt on their part.

> *Where was God in this? Why did He allow this to happen? The answer is in later chapters.*

The Lord Was With Joseph - Genesis 39:1 - 6

Verse 2 is a key verse. It says that "The Lord was with Joseph and he prospered…"

> *How can the Lord be with you and you are in the midst of a difficult situation? How can you prosper and still be a "slave"?*

Driven To Our Knees

Verses 3 - 6 tell how Joseph "prospered" while being a slave.

Are there blessings that occur in your life, in the midst of your trial; that you can point to and say, "The Lord did that", or "The Lord really blessed us this time", or "I don't know how we would have made it without the Lord"? If so, that's your evidence that "the Lord is with you".

Joseph Is Falsely Accused - Genesis 39:7-20
Now, verses 7 – 20 tell the story of how Potipher's wife lied and falsely accused Joseph of attempted rape. The result was that he was thrown in prison. (Actually this is another sign that God was with Joseph. Most slaves would have been executed, not sent to prison).

Sometimes the "unexpected" happens in life and your situation may get worse. It may not even be your fault. Someone may "do you wrong" and cause you more pain and suffering. Is God still in control in these situations? Verses 21 says, "Yes — God is still in control, even when bad things happen."

God Shows His Favor and Joseph Gets More Training - Genesis 39:22 - 23
Verses 22 - 23 tell how God showed His favor. Compare this to Gen. 39:5.

What skills did Joseph learn? What was Joseph learning to do?

Genesis Chapters 40 – 41 (Summary)
While in prison, Joseph meets two of Pharaoh's servants. Both servants have dreams one night. Joseph interprets both dreams (by the Lord) and the interpretations come to pass. One servant is killed the other is set free, restored to his former position. Joseph asks the freed servant to tell Pharaoh that he was wrongly accused and to get him out of prison. But the servant forgot Joseph for two years.

Then one night Pharaoh has two dreams and looks for someone to interpret them. The freed servant finally remembers Joseph interpreting his dream two years earlier. Joseph is called from prison and tells Pharaoh what God has told him about the meaning of the dream.

Joseph in Charge of Egypt - Genesis 41:28 - 40
In verses 28 - 32, Joseph tells Pharaoh the meaning of the dreams. Notice how in verse 32 he acknowledges God.

Driven To Our Knees

In verses 33 - 36 Joseph gives advice to Pharaoh on the best way to handle the coming years of abundance and famine. Pharaoh follows that advice and puts Joseph in charge of Egypt.

Joseph enters Pharaoh's presence as a slave and leaves with the power and authority of Pharaoh. God used the time spent in Potiphar's house and in prison to prepare Joseph for ruling Egypt. During his 13 years in captivity, Joseph spent much of that time in a leadership position. Each day prepared him for God's purpose — to run Egypt. After 13 years, he was suddenly transformed from a slave to one of the most powerful persons in that part of the world.

During your time in "prison" (your difficult situations) what is God preparing you for? What skills are you learning? How are you responding to your time in "prison"? Are you listening to what God has to say, or are you too busy complaining about your circumstances?

Key Point: How we respond to life is more important than what happens in life.

God's Ultimate Purpose Revealed - Genesis 45:4 - 7

Now another key question is:

Why did God place Joseph in that position?

The answer is found in Genesis 45:4 - 7. This scene takes place nine years after Joseph is put in charge of Egypt. There had been 7 years of plentiful crops and then two years of famine. Five more years of famine were coming. The tiny nation of Israel (seventy people) was on the verge of starvation. Joseph's brothers had come to Egypt to buy food because the famine was so great. To buy food they had to present themselves before the Egyptian ruler. They had no idea that the ruler to whom they were bowing down was the brother they had tried to kill 22 years earlier.

In chapter 45, Joseph finally reveals himself to his brothers and God's ultimate purpose. By Joseph being in that leadership position, he had the authority to settle his family in the most fertile region of Egypt, Goshen. This literally saved his family from starvation. God blessed the tiny nation of Israel and it grew to 2 to 3 million people in 400 years, at the time of Moses.

Key Point: Timing is critical to God fulfilling His goals for our lives.

Summary

God is in control. He knows all the details of our lives before it even happens. We don't. Some of his plans for our lives are fulfilled in a relatively short time. Other plans may not bear fruit until after we are with Him. That's why it is so important for us to trust Him and not get ahead of His plan. We need to "wait" on the Lord and seek his guidance. When we get clear guidance from Him, then we know how to move, when to move, and in what direction. Then we are to leave the consequences of our obedience to Him, for His glory.

Driven To Our Knees

Notes:

Driven To Our Knees

Facing Life's Challenges

Introduction
Life is full of challenges. There are times when crisis after crisis occurs and you wonder, "Where is God in all this?" He may seem like He's a million miles away. But the story of Jehoshaphat, king of Judah, shows us that how we respond to the challenges of life is critical to our overcoming those challenges, no matter what they are.

This lesson is a study of an event in the life of King Jehoshaphat during a time when he was surrounded by enemies. He did not provoke the attack. He had no where to run; no defense seemed adequate. So he did the wisest thing any of us can do in a seemingly helpless situation, and I think there is a lesson in his response for all of us.

Scriptures Used In This Lesson
2 Chronicles 20:1 - 30
2 Chronicles 17:6

Background:
Jehoshaphat was King of Judah from approximately 872 BC to 848 BC. In his early years as king, we are told that he followed the Lord. During this time he sent teachers throughout the land instructing the people on the ways of the Lord. As a result, the Lord gave him peace from his enemies. Then one day this peace was disturbed.

The Enemy Surrounds Jehoshaphat (2 Chronicles 20:1 – 2)
In these verses we are told that the enemies of Israel came to make war against Jehoshaphat. Notice that three different groups are involved: the Moabites, the Ammonites and Meunites.

There are times in our lives when all seems to be going well. Then all of a sudden trouble comes - we get a phone call that someone close has died, we are diagnosed with an illness, we find out that our spouse has lost his/her job, we find drugs in our child's room. These things may not be our fault. They may be totally out of our control. But they happen. The key to overcoming life's challenges is in how we respond to them.

Key Point: There is a difference between reacting to a situation and prayerfully responding to a situation.

Driven To Our Knees

How did you react to your last crisis? What was the first thing you did? What was the second thing? When did you finally seek the Lord?

Jehoshaphat's Response to the Crisis v.3-6

Initially Jehoshaphat was "alarmed". This is a very typical and human reaction to a crisis. But his next action was the key to the victory over his enemies. The scriptures say:

> "Alarmed, Jehoshaphat resolved to inquire of the Lord, and he proclaimed a fast for all of Judah."

Jehoshaphat *resolved* to seek the Lord for guidance. Not only that, he ordered the entire nation to pray with him.

In every situation, the first step should be for us to "inquire of the Lord". That should be our first inclination. We know that this was the inclination of Jehoshaphat's heart because in 2 Chronicles 17:6 we are told that "…his heart was devoted to the ways of the Lord…"

What is the condition of your heart? Are you devoted to "the ways of the Lord" or are you "casual" with your relationship with Him? With respect to your relationship with the Lord, are you a "full time employee" or a "part timer"? Full time employees enjoy certain rights, privileges, and benefits that part timers do not.

The condition of your heart, i.e., the depth of your relationship with the Lord is crucial to the outcome of your battle…victory or defeat. Jehoshaphat was ready to respond appropriately. During non-crisis time, he built up his relationship with the Lord. So when it was time for battle, he responded appropriately…to "inquire of the Lord". That should be the "bent" of our hearts. In crisis situations, we should find other godly people to pray with us and for us.

Analogy: Football teams today generate "scouting reports" on their opponents. This is done from pee-wee leagues to the pros. They spend the week before the game preparing for the upcoming battle. When game time comes, they are prepared. They don't have to run in confusion deciding what to do; they just exercise their game plan. We need to practice *before* game time so that we can be effective.

How much time do you prepare for "battle"? How do you prepare for battle?

Driven To Our Knees

Why Do We Have To Go Through Hard Times Anyway?

There are times when we all wonder, "Why did this have to happen? Why did God allow this? Was He angry? Was He trying to punish me? This was a cruel thing that happened and God allowed it and I'm mad!"

Certainly God has heard all this before. People have been angry with God before. So it's not anything new. So, what's up? Why is there so much "junk" going on?

The answer to this question is a study in itself, but there are several reasons:

- We live in a fallen world. Ever since the Garden of Eden, man has been in a state of decay – physically, morally, and spiritually. Man's nature is corrupt; he operates by that nature.

- Sometimes we cause our own problems. We deliberate disobey God, sound advice, or common sense.

- Sometimes God wants to bring us to a level of repentance. Repeatedly throughout the scriptures, God allowed his people to be conquered by an invader in order to bring them to repentance. They had fallen into sin, and the only way for them to willingly turn back to God was for them to get into a desperate situation.

- Sometimes God allows us to go through hard times so that we can be an example and comfort to others. If you read the life of Paul, you see a man who went through much hardship for the sake of the Gospel. Jesus even told him in advance. But from Paul's writings, millions upon millions of people have found comfort, strength, wisdom, power, and Christ himself. (See 2 Corinthians 1:3 - 4)

- God tests us. If we respond correctly, He will be glorified. Let's look at Hebrews 11. We probably have heard of the "heroes of faith" in this chapter, Abraham, Isaac, Moses, David, and others. But look at verses 35 - 38. The scriptures talk about believers, i.e., people of faith, being beaten, imprisoned, stoned and even sawed in two. The Bible says that, "the world was not worthy of them". *Remember there is a life after death that lasts for an eternity, either with or without God. Even though some of the "heroes of faith" may have suffered in their earthly lives, they have begun to spend an eternity in peace and joy with the Lord.*

- God is sovereign. Our parents didn't explain every decision they made concerning our welfare. We don't explain every decision or action to our children. Our children have to yield to our sovereignty just as we did to our parents. We have to yield to the sovereignty of an all powerful, all loving God, in whom we can fully trust.

Key Elements of Jehoshaphat's Prayer v. 6 – 12

1. Verse 6 acknowledges who God is…His sovereignty, power and might.
2. Verses 7 – 8 are reminders of the great things God has done. Do you keep a personal journal of what God has done in our life? *Why not document your testimony?*
3. Verse 9 declares Jehoshaphat's dependence on God.
4. Verses 10 – 11 finally state the problem. Notice where this falls in the order of the prayer.
5. Verse 12 states their determination to focus on Him.

The Battle is Not Yours But God's v. 14 – 17

God answers the sincere, heartfelt prayer of Jehoshaphat (See James 5:16). He encourages Jehoshaphat and tells him something we should always keep in mind, "…For the battle is not yours, but God's."

When the battle is God's, we are to leave the circumstances to Him. He is responsible for our well-being and the outcome. Our job is to trust and obey. If the situation is out of your control anyway, what else can you do? You might as well trust and obey. This is how God gets glory.

As The Praises Go Up… v. 21 – 22

Jehoshaphat did an interesting thing in his preparation for battle…he appointed men to sing to the Lord and to praise Him for "the splendor of His holiness". This wasn't necessarily a feeling he had…he *chose* to praise the Lord. In the midst of our trials, we should *choose* to praise God. Our praise may be in the form of acknowledging his greatness or the things He did for us in the past. But some form of praise is crucial to our victory over our circumstances.

Verse 22 states that as they began to sing, the Lord set an ambush against their enemies. God often works "behind the scenes", in ways we cannot imagine. We should never underestimate the power of our God.

> **The Keys To Jehoshaphat's Prayer and Victory**
>
> - Acknowledging Who God Is
> - Remind yourself of what He has done in the past
> - Declare your dependence on God
> - Tell Him your need
> - Determine to stay focused on Him

Driven To Our Knees

The Victory v. 24 – 26

Jehoshaphat and the nation of Judah did not have to lift a sword. The battle was already won by the time they arrived on the battlefield. God even blessed them with so much plunder that it took three days to collect it all.

Summary

What God will do in our moment of crisis will depend on our response and His overall plan for our lives. The response of Jehoshaphat to the impending destruction of his nation and his prayer should be models for us to follow the next time we face the challenges of life. Begin to pray like Jehoshaphat; 1) Acknowledge Who God Is first, 2) Remind yourself of the things He has done for you in the past, 3) Declare your dependence on God; you need Him; you can't do it by yourself, 4) Tell Him your need, 5) State your determination to stay focused on Him.

Driven To Our Knees

Notes:

Driven To Our Knees

How To Know The Voice of God

Introduction

Two of the most common questions in a Christian's life are: "How do I know I'm hearing the voice of God? What does His voice sound like?" These are simple questions, but so crucial to everyday living. This lesson focuses on answering these questions so that you can receive the guidance, encouragement and blessings that God has for you on a daily basis.

Scriptures Used In This Lesson

Psalm 81:8 – 16
I Kings 19:11 - 13
I Samuel 3:1 – 10
Ephesians 4:30
Genesis 12:1 - 4
Proverbs 12:15
Judges 6:1 - 39

God Wants To Talk To Us

The first thing in hearing the voice of God is to know that God still speaks to His people and wants to communicate with us. In Psalm 81:8 – 16 we see how God mentions that His people would not listen to Him, three times. We can see that God strongly desires for us to listen. Think of a loving father who's trying to give his teenage son some advice. He has that strong desire for Him to listen because he cares and wants the best for his son. But when the son goes his own way, the father feels disappointed. This is the emotion in this passage, but only stronger. God's love for us is immeasurably more intense. So know that God wants to speak to us.

How Does He Speak?

In the Bible we can see that God spoke to His people in a number of ways:

- Directly in an audible voice
- Directly in a still quiet voice
- Through animals
- Through circumstances
- By His Spirit
- Through the life of Christ
- In dreams
- In visions

- Through angels
- Through prophets
- Through the Bible
- Strong impressions

God can use any means to communicate with us, but the primary ways He communicates today are:

- Through His Word (the Bible)
- By His Spirit

The Bible and The Holy Spirit work hand and hand. As we prayerfully read His Word, we get in a frame of mind where we are focused on God. It's like picking up the phone and dialing His number. Then as we read and mediate on His Word, His Spirit brings things to mind. He provides answers to questions we have; sometimes it's through the passage we are reading; sometimes it just comes to mind as we read. The Holy Spirit enlightens us. It's like helping your child work an algebra problem for 20 minutes and finally you get the problem to work. You say, "Ah, that's it!"

Key Point: God can communicate in a number of ways, but primarily, He communicates through His Word and His Spirit.

What does His voice sound like? Well it varies. Sometimes it's a clear audible voice. This can happen, but not as often as we read in the Word. Most often it's a "still small voice". In I Kings 19:11 - 13, Elijah didn't hear God in the earthquake or strong wind, but in the "still small voice".

Now why is this? Have you ever been in your house and had a radio blasting, the TV on, and had some people talking in the other room? In order to read the paper or a magazine, you had "tune out" all the distractions in order to hear yourself read. It was easy to lose concentration and focus on all the other voices around you.

Now, have you ever been in the same house by yourself, with no TV or radio on? You can hear the house crack or the wind blowing down the chimney. Do these sounds only occur when the house is empty? No, they happen all the time, but you miss these sounds because of all the other distractions. God speaks to us "quietly" so we can learn to be still. He wants us "quiet" and "still" so we can focus on Him, and Him alone. He doesn't want us distracted. When we are still, we are more attuned to His voice. We are more focused. When we are still, we are more apt to listen to Him.

Driven To Our Knees

Its All About Relationship

The main desire of God is to have an intimate relationship with us. That's why He sent His Son – to restore the relationship between God and man. Now in order to hear his voice, several things need to be in order. First, we need to be humble and willing to listen. In I Samuel 3:1 – 10, Samuel was a young child when he was placed under the care of Eli the priest of Israel. This was the beginning of Samuel's training as a priest. His ultimate job was to be the "voice of God" to the people. God would talk to Samuel and Samuel would tell the people what God had told him. Samuel's response the third time the Lord speaks to him is an example of the attitude we should have – one of humility and a willingness to be obedient. Notice that Samuel didn't recognize God's voice immediately; it was a learning process.

Key Point: Hearing the voice of God is a learning process.

> *Have you ever thought you were hearing from God about a situation, but later realized that it was just your own desire? Did you use that occasion to learn to sift through your voice verse God's?*

Sometimes when God speaks you know immediately who it is. In Genesis 12:1 – 4, Abraham knew immediately that it was God speaking to him, instructing him to leave his land and family and travel to a land that He would show him. But most of the time for us, God's voice is not that clear; we must learn to recognize His voice.

Now, why is this? It's all about relationship – as we strive to recognize God's voice, we build our relationship with Him.

Several things happen as we strive to recognize His voice:

- We become more focused on Him
- We spend more time seeking Him
- Our minds spend more time thinking about Him and godly things
- Our desire for Him grows

And all these work to build our relationship with Him. Think of it in terms of your spouse (or spouse to be). As the above four points occurred in your relationship with your spouse, you all got closer. After a while, you didn't have to identify yourself when you called on the phone – your spouse "knew" your voice. (No caller ID required).

Driven To Our Knees

Key Point: The more time you spend with God, the more you'll be able to recognize His voice; it will become easier over time.

Wise Counsel

There are times when you need to seek wise, godly counsel in order help you know if the voice you're hearing is that of God. Proverbs 12:15 instructs us to seek wise counsel, but I must interject a few words of caution:

- The counsel must be from a spirit filled, saved, godly person. "Nick the Wino" most likely will not provide godly counsel.
- The person from whom you seek counsel, must not have preconceived ideas or another agenda.
- Sometimes God won't tell someone else what He wants you to know. He wants to develop a relationship with you *directly*.
- Don't depend on that person to hear from God for you all the time. Again, God wants YOU.
- *God's spoken word will never contradict His written word. God doesn't contradict Himself. If someone tells you something contrary to principals found in the Bible, it's not from God.*

Throwing Out A Fleece

Read about Gideon in Judges 6:1 – 39. Throwing out a fleece was not and is not a sign of faith. So it is not the primary way God wants to speak to us. But there are times when we don't know what to do, and God will direct the circumstances in our lives in order to show us His will. This leads to another point:

Key Point: God will confirm His Word to you.

Be assured that God will confirm His Word to help you be more confident in knowing His voice.

> *Can you think of a time when God confirmed His Word to you through circumstances?*

You May Not Like What You Hear

God sometimes tells us to do some things which may contradict common sense, or may cause loved ones to question us, or may upset some people, or be the opposite of what you want to do. Abraham was instructed to sacrifice his son Isaac, through whom God promised Abraham would have many decedents. You need to have an attitude of obedience, submissiveness, and trust in His *ability and character*.

Driven To Our Knees

Has God ever told you to do something that was "difficult", but worked out in the end?

Again, it's all about relationship – building that trusting, loving, fruitful relationship with the Creator of all things. There is only one person who was called "God's friend" and that was Abraham (Isaiah 41:8, James 2:23, 2 Chronicles 20:7). We are His "children" because we have His nature, His "DNA" inside us – the Holy Spirit. That's how close He wants to be.

Keys To Successful Listening

1. Think about His Word after you read it throughout the day, i.e., meditate on it
2. Listen expectantly, that you *will* hear from Him
3. Be quiet
4. Be patient; there's a right time for Him to fulfill His Word
5. Be confident God will tell us what we need to hear at that moment
6. Be in right relationship; Don't grieve His Spirit; Ephesians 4: 30
7. He sometimes speak through your circumstances
8. Be honest with yourself; don't rationalize your sin; if you're just trying to satisfy a fleshly desire, then its probably not God
9. You may not like what you hear, but trust Him
10. Be submissive
11. Make sure what you hear is consistent with the word of God
12. Be aware that sometimes His instructions will conflict with human reasoning
13. When He speaks, it may challenge your faith (Gen. 12:1)
14. Does it call for an act of courage
15. God won't rush; there is a right time for everything. But when He says, "Move", you better move.
16. God will glorify Himself
17. It will contribute to your spiritual growth

Summary

Hearing God's voice is a learning process that will contribute to your spiritual growth, build your relationship with Him, and give God glory. It is one of the most important things you can learn to do as a Christian. Why not start today by asking God to help you hear his voice and be obedient to His will? If you already hear His voice, ask Him to help you grow in the knowledge and understanding of Him.

Notes:

Driven To Our Knees

God's Word: Can I Live By It?

Introduction

In Deuteronomy we are told that "man does not live on bread alone, but by every word that comes from the mouth of the Lord" (Deut. 8:3, NIV). Jesus quotes this verse in the book of Matthew when He is being tempted by Satan. Psalm 119 (the longest chapter in the book of Psalms) has as its primary focus God's Word. What is it about God's Word that makes It so significant and powerful. How is it that I can live "by every word that comes from the mouth of the Lord"? How is it that His Word has the ability to sustain me? What does that mean to me in my daily life?

A close study of some key verses in Psalm 119 provides some insight into the power of God's word.

Scriptures for This Lesson
Psalm 119:89 – 96
Genesis 15:4 – 5, 12 - 15

His Word is Eternally Established

Verse 89 establishes a key characteristic of God's Word: it is strong enough to be the foundation of our lives. In the KJV, the word "settled" comes from the Hebrew word "niphal" which means to stand firm, to station one's self, to take an upright position. This verse also says that His Word is eternal. So God's Word is firmly established forever; it does not shift or change.

When you think about this, think about Mount Everest. The mountain existed 2000 years ago, standing firm and majestic at over 29,000 ft tall, and will be there 2000 years from now. His Word is firm; It is eternal; It does not fade. It is strong enough to serve as a foundation for our lives. Something that is eternally established, is what's needed to be the "foundation" of our lives.

> *Can you think of anything else that can serve as a foundation for our lives, something that we can live our lives by? How about laws, fame, fortune, material possessions?*

Another illustration comes to mind when I think of God's Word being our foundation. I used to live in West Texas for a number of years. When I was having a house built, the builder needed to pour a concrete slab to serve as the foundation of the house. After digging about 8 inches into the ground, the builder ran into caliche; basically a limestone rock formation underneath the thin topsoil. Caliche is so hard and solid that the builder had to use a jack hammer in order to complete the foundation. My house was built on solid ground. It was not going to "settle" or shift. It was firmly established.

Driven To Our Knees

God's Word is like the caliche of West Texas. Its nature is that it is firm, solid, and established. If we use it as the foundation for our lives, we don't have to worry about our lives shifting.

God Keeps His Word

Verse 90 illustrates another characteristic of His Word: faithfulness. Because His Word is eternal and firm, you can depend it. By definition, His Word is faithful.

When you think of God's Word being "faithful unto all generations", think of God's promise to Abraham. In Genesis 15:4 – 5, and 12 – 15, the Lord makes a promise to Abraham saying that, 1) he would have descendants as numerous as the stars in heaven, and 2) they would be enslaved for 400 years. God told Abraham this around 2100 BC.

Two hundred years later, around 1900 BC, Joseph is betrayed by his brothers and is taken to Egypt as a slave. After 13 years, he rises to become second-in-command in Egypt next to Pharaoh. He brings his family to Egypt, and they remain there for 400 years. During that time, the Hebrews are enslaved by the Egyptians, but their numbers grow. By the time Moses delivers them from bondage (around 1500 BC), the Hebrew population had grown to about 2 to 3 million people.

The fact that 600 years passed between the time God spoke to Abraham and Moses delivered the people, didn't diminish the faithfulness of God's Word. His Word was faithful through all of Abraham's generations.

> *Can you think of a time in your life when God spoke to you or someone else and it was quite a while before it was fulfilled? What did you think when God first told you? What did you think when it finally came to pass?*

The second half of verse 90 states that God established the earth, and it endures. Another way to look at it is that the earth endures because God established it. This expresses His power and sovereignty over all things.

God is Sovereign

Verse 91 continues the idea of the sovereignty of God's Word. Notice that all things serve Him - not a few, not many, not most, but all things.

Verse 92 caught my attention as I was reading this Psalm.

> "If your law had not been my delight, I would have perished in my affliction."

As I thought about what this meant, I began to realize the very power of God's Word. To have God's Word as your "delight" means that you think about His Word often. You have It on your mind constantly. It gives you joy and contentment to think about It. Dwelling on Him opens the lines of communication to God. As a result, you respond appropriately to different situations in life. You hear from God when you really need to. The Lord keeps you when you're in a stressful situation. As a result, you avoid "perishing in your affliction". God's Word Saves.

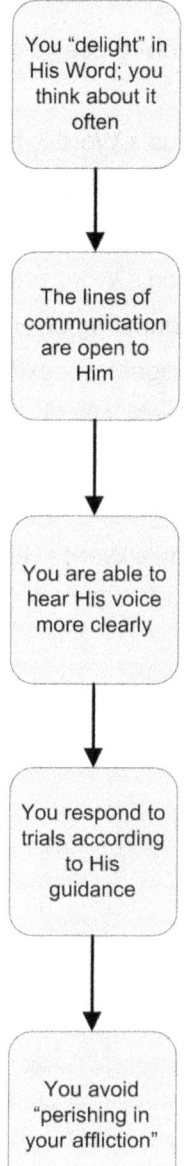

Can you think of a time when after you read His Word you felt in touch with God? How did you respond to people and situations immediately afterward? Did it make a difference?

Verse 93 is a continuation of the idea that God's Word Saves.

Seek His Word Diligently
In verse 94, the word "sought" comes from the Hebrew word "darash" which means to seek with care, to seek God in prayer, to seek with a demand or requirement, to investigate, to enquire. The verb is active instead of passive. So the idea is not to superficially seek God, but to diligently and earnestly seek Him with expectation; to read His Word with a demand, a requirement to know Him more. If you seek Him with all your heart, you will find Him.

Keeping His Word On Your Mind
Verse 95 is also interesting. When the wicked are waiting to destroy you, it doesn't say, "Prepare for battle" or "Devise a plan to protect yourself or to get even with them". The Word says to "ponder on His statues".

Certainly God doesn't want us destroyed; He loves us too much. So why would He say, "ponder on His statues"? Because His Word is just that important and that powerful. The victory will come through His Word. Nothing else can save like His Word. It's the first place to start, not the last. So when trouble surrounds you, ponder, dwell on God's Word.

Driven To Our Knees

God's Word Has No Limits

The simple message of verse 96 is that *God's Word Has No Limits*. So His Word is adequate; It can handle every situation that comes our way...every one. There are no limits.

Summary

As we review these verses, we have discovered:

1. God's Word is firmly established. Therefore It can be the foundation of our lives.
2. His Word doesn't shift with time; It is constant.
3. God is faithful. No matter how much time passes, God will keep His Word.
4. God's Word is sovereign. His Word sustains the world.
5. Pondering on His Word can save me.
6. Diligently seeking God's Word saves me.
7. God's Word has no limits.

Based on all this, is there any legitimate reason to doubt Him in any situation? Let's begin today to trust in God's Word. His Word keeps you alive.

Driven To Our Knees

Notes:

Driven To Our Knees

Driven To Our Knees

Introduction

There are times when things happen in our lives where we become very much aware that "life is hard". Sickness, death, car accidents, layoffs, robberies, and the like, all come crashing into our lives. We look around us and other people seem to be immune from such tragedies...and these are the ungodly people. We wonder, "Why me?" and "Where's God?", and "What is going on?"

This lesson is a study of a man who experienced an almost fatal test of faith. He looks around and sees the ungodly prospering. He struggled in his faith and his understanding of God. And from his reflections, we can learn how to properly respond to life's situations when we are "driven to our knees".

Scriptures Used In This Lesson

Psalm 73
2 Corinthians 5:15 – 21
Colossians 1:22
James 5:16
Psalm 27
Psalm 37:25 –28, 39 - 40

Background

Psalm 73 is attributed to Asaph, leader of one of David's three Levitical choirs. The Levites were descendants of Levi, one of Jacob's (Israel's) sons, and were chosen by God to be priests. We are not told specifically what issues were plaguing Asaph, but it is obvious that his faith had been tested.

God is Good, But Woe is Me — v.1 - 2

In these verses we can see how Asaph attempts to encourage himself by affirming how God has been good to Israel. But we can see that he feels that he has missed out on God's blessings.

Look At Those Folks Over There — v.3 - 5

In these verses Asaph looks around him and he sees the ungodly flourishing. He sees:

- The prosperity of the wicked
- They have no struggles
- They are free from burdens common to man
- Free from "human ills" (NIV)

Driven To Our Knees

Now based on your experience and understanding of life, is there anyone who "never" experiences something "bad"? Has there been anyone who "never" got sick? Of course not. Everyone has problems of some sort. A grandparent dies, someone gets laid off from their job, and so on. But when we are in the midst of our storm, the outside world seems calm to us.

Is The Grass Greener Or Are There Weeds On the Other Side of The Fence?
Before we address the next few verses in this Psalm, I want to review Christ's purpose here on earth. Read the following scriptures.

2 Corinthians 5:15 – 21
Colossians 1:22

Reconcile – katallasso

1. to change, exchange, as coins for others of equivalent value
    a. to reconcile (those who are at variance)
    b. return to favor with, be reconciled to one
    c. to receive one into favor

Notice the first part of the definition…"to exchange as coins for others of equivalent value". Jesus is our substitute. We switched places with Him. Christ took our place on the cross and we took His, being reconciled to God our Father. When we accepted Christ as our savior and Lord, we achieved an equivalent value to Christ in His eye; God is Jesus' Father, and ours. We are "returned to favor" with God.

So Christ came to restore the relationship between God and man. Anything that diminishes that relationship undermines the work of Christ. It puts us in a state of separation from God. Now let's continue on with Psalm 73. Read Psalm 73:6 – 12

Let's look at what happens when life is easy:

- Verse 6 – pride and violence
- Verse 7 – callous hearts, iniquity (gross injustice, wickedness, sin), evil thoughts with no limits
- Verse 8 – scoff and speak with malice (destroying someone's character, reputation), arrogant, threaten others
- Verse 9 – they want all that they see (covet), no recognition of God

Driven To Our Knees

- Verse 10 – they take all that belongs to them and then some; they are wasteful
- Verse 11 – they dishonor, and disrespect God

Think of a child who is spoiled; everything goes their way. What kind of tendencies will they develop? Think of our nation; how would we be as a nation if everything was easy?

Below is a quote from Theodore Roosevelt, president of the United States from 1901 – 1909:

> "The things that will destroy America are prosperity at any price, peace at any price, safety first instead of duty first, the love of soft living and the get rich quick theory of life."
>
> *Do you think Theodore Roosevelt's quote is accurate concerning the United States? Why or Why not? Why do you think people fall away from God when life is easy? What does this say about our nature? What does it take to get us "back in line"?*

Man has an inherently corrupt nature. If left alone, without restraints or correction, our true nature would be displayed. Verses 6 – 11 tell us what we are really like.

But God's desire for us to have an intimate relationship with Him is so strong, that we gradually take on His character traits. Sometimes He allows things to happen in our lives to "drive us to our knees" so that we seek Him; we eventually get back in right fellowship with Him. It is through Christ that this relationship can be restored.

Key Point: The pains of life are what God uses to draw us closer to Him.

Key Point: The key to overcoming any obstacle in life is how we respond to that obstacle, no matter how painful.

Let's continue to get a sense of the pain of Asaph. Read verses 13 – 14, 21 – 22. Asaph's pain was real, as is yours. Sometimes we are at the point of despair. But, where are you going to go? Who are you going to turn to? Asaph asked these questions and came up with one answer. It's given in verses 23 – 26.

There is no place to go, but God. There is no real hope, but God. Even if the consequences of life are not at all what you wanted, He is the only hope you have in overcoming your trials.

Driven To Our Knees

When you're "driven to your knees", you pray more intensely; you become more honest with yourself and God. Your prayers become more effective. Your relationship with Him gets closer. Let's remember how we're supposed to pray. Read James 5:16.

James says that when our prayer is heartfelt, sincere, and intense, it can do much and becomes powerful and effective. Will it change our circumstances? Maybe, maybe not. But you will change and get closer to God. As we get closer to God, the purpose of Christ's death (to reconcile man to God) becomes fulfilled.

Hope

Through all the "soul searching", Asaph comes to a conclusion about his life. There is no other place to go but in the arms of our loving Heavenly Father. Read verses 27 – 28.

Here is the hope that we have; read Psalm 27.

Psalm 37:25 – 28 and 39 – 40 have been especially encouraging to me over the years.

> ^{25} I was young and now I am old,
> yet I have never seen the righteous forsaken
> or their children begging bread.
> ^{26} They are always generous and lend freely;
> their children will be blessed.
>
> ^{27} Turn from evil and do good;
> then you will dwell in the land forever.
> ^{28} For the LORD loves the just
> and will not forsake his faithful ones.
>
> ^{39} The salvation of the righteous comes from the LORD;
> he is their stronghold in time of trouble.
> ^{40} The LORD helps them and delivers them;
> he delivers them from the wicked and saves them,
> because they take refuge in him.

Driven To Our Knees

Summary

How you respond to the issues of life determine how victorious we will be in life. When driven to your knees, turn to God. Remember that on your knees, you are in perfect position to receive His love, His comfort, His understanding and all the benefits that come with knowing the Creator of all things.

Driven To Our Knees

Notes:

Driven To Our Knees

Overcoming Obstacles

Introduction
Life is full of obstacles. They seem to multiply especially when you are close to acquiring a goal or blessing God has given you. When you are on a mission from God and the opposition seems insurmountable, press on with God, not on your own strength. God's word cannot change. If we press on and not give up, we will receive blessings and leave a testimony that will amaze others.

Scriptures for This Lesson
Nehemiah 2
Nehemiah 4
Nehemiah 6
Psalm 62:1 - 2, 5 - 8

Background
This lesson revolves around events in the life of Nehemiah, about 445 BC. Nehemiah, a servant of King Artaxerxes, hears about the condition of the city of Jerusalem. The city had been devastated and reduced to a pile of rubble, due to decades of conquest and neglect. Israel's continuous sin had caused them to be conquered and deported by King Nebuchadnezzar 70 years earlier. Nehemiah hears details of the city in ruin and the news breaks his heart. He mourns, fasts, and prays for several days. He finally prays that God would give him favor as he approaches the King to request permission to return to Jerusalem and rebuild God's sacred city.

The Obstacles
As with any major project there are obstacles to overcome. In Nehemiah's case, the obstacles seemed overwhelming; enough to discourage anyone from taking on the task. But, God had placed such a burden on Nehemiah heart to rebuild the city that he had to act. The return of the exiles to the city was a fulfillment of God's word given 70 years earlier (Jeremiah 25:8 - 14).

Obvious obstacles were the following:

- There was no protection for the inhabitants of the city who were starting to come back. The wall around the city had been completely destroyed.
- Nehemiah had to find enough workers to complete the work.
- Food, water, shelter, supplies, and clothing had to be provided for all the workers for an extended period of time.
- They needed to have construction plans.

Driven To Our Knees

- Initially, Nehemiah was in Babylon, 600 miles from Jerusalem. He and his companions had to make a long and dangerous journey.

Key Point: When God ordains a project, He will provide what is needed to get it done. He may provide tangible resources, but keep in mind that He will also provide intangible resources such as courage, wisdom, special knowledge, and guidance by the Holy Spirit.

Can you think of other intangible resources that God may provide to accomplish His plan for your life or the life of someone you know?

Nehemiah was the cupbearer for King Artaxerxes. It was four months between the time he first heard about the condition of Jerusalem and the time he approached the King. As a servant, he was to keep his personal feelings to himself, no matter what his problems were. Immediately Nehemiah faced two more obstacles:

- How to approaching the King with a personal problem, without being put in prison or put to death.
- Getting the King to say "Yes".

In verses 2:1 – 2, the King's response is very revealing. By asking, "Why does your heart look so sad...", it shows that Nehemiah had gained some level of favor with the King. Nehemiah had obviously performed his duties well and had established a good reputation with Artaxerxes. Obviously he was someone the King felt could be trusted and someone he cared about personally. Nehemiah's previous work performance and character established the foundation for a favorable response, well before he heard about Jerusalem's condition. This foundation is what God used to perform His will, the rebuilding of Jerusalem through Nehemiah.

Key Point: Laying down a good foundation is crucial to overcoming obstacles. Establishing a good foundation involves: 1) a growing personal relationship with Jesus Christ through prayer and study, 2) being a man/woman of integrity, 3) working hard, 4) taking care of yourself physically, 5) getting training, skills or special knowledge, 6) establishing positive relationships with others who may assist you later on.

What kind of foundation have you laid down at work? At home? At church? Can God use it to accomplish a special goal in your life?

Driven To Our Knees

Another key verse is v.3. Nehemiah overcame his fear and took a step of courage/faith and told the King his concern. This could have meant his death, but the need was great.

Key Point: Sometimes we have to overcome a fear in order to overcome an obstacle. Fear may come as feelings of reluctance, being uncomfortable, or just being afraid.

Verse 4 is another revealing verse. When the King asked, "What is it you want?", that indicated that God had opened the door to the fulfillment of His word. God had worked in the mind and heart of an unbelieving king (i.e., he did not worship Jehovah God) to give Nehemiah the favor he needed.

Key Point: Don't underestimate God. He can work with anybody, at any time without you knowing what's going on, to accomplish His purpose – even through the ungodly.

Can you think of a time in your life where God worked through an unsaved person to give you favor or accomplish a goal in your life?

Nehemiah's relationship with God is revealed again in this passage by the fact that he prayed *before* he answered the king. A wise person will pray before he/she responds in a critical situation.

Just Because — Nehemiah 2:10

Verse 10 tells of how Sanballat, and Tobiah were "very much disturbed about Nehemiah's arrival to "promote the welfare of the Israelites". Sanballat was the governor of Samaria, just 12 miles away. Tobiah was an Ammonite (half Jew). Their opposition to Nehemiah's arrival was probably based on seeing Nehemiah as a political threat. They might have seen Nehemiah as a new "acting governor" who could threaten their realm of power.

Sometimes you won't find a "good" reason for an obstacle in your life. Some people will oppose you "just because". Some people will be jealous or feel threatened by your success "just because". Their reasons for opposition will be more personal and based on emotion as opposed to a specific problem.

Key Point: There will almost always be opposition to a movement of God. Satan does not want God to receive the glory.

More Attacks on the Work of God — Nehemiah 4

Have you ever had someone "just talk bad" about you? Spread lies? Belittling everything you do? That is what is revealed in Nehemiah 4:1 – 3. Saballat and Tobiah seemed to be having a "field day"

Driven To Our Knees

"doggin'" the work of the Jews. What's interesting is that upon hearing of progress of the rebuilding of the wall, they were extremely angry. The KJV version says that they "took great indignation".

Satan hates God, and hates His children. He becomes angry at any move, blessing, or progress of God. This "great indignation" is seen in Saballat and Tobiah.

Key Point: Be aware that your successes for God will make some people jealous, angry, or resentful.

But notice Nehemiah's prayer in verses 4 – 5, he asks the Lord *not* to blot out their sins, he wanted them held accountable for their actions. Truly ungodly or *unrepentant* people will not stop until you are destroyed. So is the case in verse 8. What's interesting is Nehemiah's response. He protects himself, day and night (verse 4:16, 21 - 23). Half of the men protect the project and the other half perform the work.

Key Point: Prayer (protection) must be continuous while the work of God is being conducted.

What this passage also says is that we have to be ever mindful of our unrepentant enemies. Do not show them any slack, because at the first opportunity, they will destroy you and the work God has called you to do. We have to be always alert and watchful for their deceit, words of discouragement (v. 4:12), and their underhanded plots. Do not trust your unrepentant enemies.

What are the weapons of our warfare? What is your first line of defense or attack?

Nehemiah presses on with the work of God. Verse 4:14 shows how he encouraged the people of God. He tells them to: 1) not be afraid, 2) remember the Lord who is great and awesome, and 3) fight for the ones you love. Nehemiah was fighting the battle of the mind. He was giving his people something else to think about other than the enemy and his might.

In overcoming obstacles, we must focus on the positive, the power and awesomeness of a God who loves us; who continually blesses us in numerous ways. David encouraged himself by focusing on the Lord (Psalm 62:1 - 2, 5 - 8).

Key Point: Satan's primary area of attack against the Christian is the mind. If he can get you to focus on anything else but God, then he can keep you from receiving your blessing and God receiving glory.

Driven To Our Knees

Do you encourage yourself in the Lord? Why or why not? Why don't we do it more often?

Notice verse 12 again. The Jews who came to Nehemiah were totally focused on "the problem", i.e., on the opposition. They spoke words of defeat. Nehemiah had to reverse their thinking and take action. Since the people were speaking defeat, Nehemiah had to show them that they would be protected.

More Deceit — Nehemiah 6

After the wall was complete, Nehemiah's enemies still tried to deceive him so they could kill him. They tried repeatedly. Again, the ungodly, unrepentent mind is bent on your destruction, even after he's lost the battle. Always watch your back.

Summary

Achieving the goals of God brings glory to Him in the eyes of others. Verses 15 – 16 show that God was glorified in the midst of His enemies. Nehemiah's persistence provided an amazing testimony. So it is with us. If we press on, and are watchful of our enemies, we will receive the blessing. We will accomplish the goals of God. With God on our side, and our faithful obedience, no obstacle will stand in our way – it will crumble – we cannot lose.

Driven To Our Knees

Notes:

Driven To Our Knees

God is Good

Introduction

God is good. This is a true statement. We've all heard it before. But what does it mean? When bad things happen to us or we go through a prolonged illness or trial, is God still good? When men fly a hijacked airplane into a building and kill thousands of people, is God still good? When we tragically lose a loved one, is God still good?

The single answer to all these questions is "Yes — He is good." But we need dig a little deeper into what we mean by "good". This lesson is designed to help us better understand the goodness of God; to understand that the attributes of His character never change.

Scriptures Used In This Lesson
Mark 10:18
Matthew 7:15 – 20
Psalm 23
James 1:2 – 4, 12
II Corinthians 1:3 – 5
James 1:5 – 8

What Does "Good" Mean?

To help us obtain a better understand of the "goodness of God", we need to first define what we mean by "good".

In the dictionary, there are over 30 entries for the word "good". The word is used as an adjective (describing a noun), an adverb (describing an action/verb), and as a noun. With all these different uses in our language, it is easy to get confused over what the word means when we use it in reference to God.

In the book of Genesis, the "good" that God uses to describe His work during creation is "towb", which means the following:

1. good, pleasant, agreeable
    good, excellent (of its kind)
    good, rich, valuable in estimation
    good, appropriate, becoming
    glad, happy, prosperous (of man's sensuous nature)

good, kind, benign

good, right (ethical) n m

2. a good thing, benefit, welfare

   welfare, prosperity, happiness

   good things (collective)

   good, benefit

   moral good n f

3. welfare, benefit, good things

   welfare, prosperity, happiness

   good things (collective)

   bounty

All of these definitions are appropriate for describing the work God did during creation. We are sustained and gain our wellbeing and happiness by His creations everyday — even with every breath.

In Mark 10:18, Jesus says:

> And Jesus said unto him, Why callest thou me **good**? There is none **good** but one, that is, **God**.

"Good" in this verse comes from the Greek word "agathos" which means:

- of good constitution or nature
- useful, salutary
- good, pleasant, agreeable, joyful, happy
- excellent, distinguished
- upright, honorable

All of these attributes speak of God's character, and it is because of His character that "good" or "towb" flows into our lives; or goodness (towb) is the "fruit" of God's character (agathos).

Let's take a look at Matthew 7:15 – 20:

> "Watch out for false prophets. They come to you in sheep's clothing, but inwardly they are ferocious wolves. By their fruit you will recognize them. Do people pick grapes from thorn bushes, or figs from thistles? Likewise every good tree bears good fruit, but a bad tree bears bad fruit. A good tree cannot bear bad fruit, and a bad tree

cannot bear good fruit. Every tree that does not bear good fruit is cut down and thrown into the fire. Thus, by their fruit you will recognize them. (NIV)

Jesus taught us a basic principle about the "fruit" of our lives and we can apply it to the character of our Father. "Good" things flow to us from God because that is His nature; that is the only type of fruit He can produce.

When we combine "towb" and "agathos", *we see that because God is excellent, distinguished, upright and honorable, He produces things that are rich, excellent, appropriate, happy, right and beneficial.* It's His nature to do so.

How does that translate to our daily lives? Well, when I looked at my own life, I could clearly see the goodness of God in every situation.

When I Sinned
Recently, I became more keenly aware of my sins against God. I thought of times when I was disobedient, selfish; when I didn't trust Him; when I did something I knew I shouldn't do, but did it anyway…just out of rebellion.

But God, out of his infinite goodness, blessed me anyway. The fact that I have been given another day to seek a closer relationship with Him indicates that He is "good". Because of His good nature, He forgave me, and treated me as if the things I did that separated me from Him, didn't exist at all. He "washed" them away. Because of His "agathos", I received the "towb", i.e., forgiveness.

Key Point: God's forgiveness is a fruit of His goodness.

When I Suffered Hurt
Everyone will suffer pain in life; emotional pain, physical pain, or both. It's a fact of our fallen world. We all have lost someone very close to us. Some of us have been the victim of a crime. Some of us have suffered greatly at the hands of others, at no fault of our own.

At all times, under all conditions, God has been there to carry me through the situation. One of the most famous Psalms speaks of God's goodness through the storm:

> The LORD is my shepherd, I shall not be in want.
> He makes me lie down in green pastures,
> he leads me beside quiet waters,

he restores my soul.
He guides me in paths of righteousness
for his name's sake.
Even though I walk
through the valley of the shadow of death,
I will fear no evil,
for you are with me;
your rod and your staff,
they comfort me.
You prepare a table before me
in the presence of my enemies.
You anoint my head with oil;
my cup overflows.
Surely goodness and love will follow me
all the days of my life,
and I will dwell in the house of the LORD
forever.

Verse 4 says that "...I *walk* through the valley of the shadow of death, I will fear no evil". First of all, some of our trials may last a long time, at least from our point of view. Our desire is to *run* through the "valley of the shadow of death" not walk. But as we walk, we learn to persevere. In James 1:2 – 4, 12, we see the value of perseverance.

Also the verse acknowledges that we will go *through* the valley – not around, or under, or above, but *through* the valley. But these valley experiences, although painful, have value. Read II Corinthians 1:3 – 5. Our valley experiences allow us to comfort, encourage, and support others. God can use us to minister to others in a most effective way. Our testimony of how God blessed us through the trials have a high level of credibility because "we've been there", we "*know* what's going on". As a result God's blessings to us are *multiplied* because we pass them on to others.

The verse also says that I will fear no evil. Why? Because He is with me. It tells me that some storms God will allow us to experience. And when He does, we have the opportunity to see another side of His "agathos". His "goodness" is displayed by lovingly carrying us through the storm. People will comfort us with the right words at the right time. A blessing will seemingly come from nowhere. We gain the ability to comfort others going through similar situations.

Driven To Our Knees

The key to experiencing God's goodness through the storm is in our response to the storm. The Psalm says that, "...I will fear no evil". If we walk in faith and not fear, we will experience His goodness. The "towb" of His goodness will be His peace and comfort through the storm. In the times that I have *chosen* to trust Him, He has never let me down.

Key Point: How we respond to trials will determine the fruit that we will receive.

How has God "carried" you recently? What fruit have you received? Did you pass it on?

I Should Have Died

One of the things that amazes my wife is how I've stayed alive while driving. She jokes with me on occasions saying, "I *know* God is watching over you." She jokes, but the statement is true.

One winter night after leaving a restaurant, we were driving westbound along Interstate 70 in Missouri. I looked back in my rear view mirror and noticed someone cutting across all the lanes of the westbound traffic. They must have been traveling 90 to 100 miles per hour. Then suddenly they lost control, slid off the road, spun around and stopped in the ditch between the highway and the service road, pointing east. The car they cut off slid off the road, across the median and stopped on the service road. Fortunately no cars were on the service road or there would have been a collision.

I told my wife about it as we exited off the highway. If we had been 5 seconds later leaving the restaurant, we would have been the victims of the foolish driver.

We've all had experiences like this. It was only the goodness of God, His grace, that kept us alive and from harm. I had no control over the situation. I didn't know someone would be driving recklessly, on that highway, at that time. But God protected us. He protects us daily from dangers, seen and unseen. He does this not because we deserve it, but because He is good.

Key Point: The fruit of God's goodness is His grace and protection.

How has God saved you recently, or shown you His grace?

He Blessed Me in Ways I Could Not Have Imagined

After my family and I moved to St. Louis from Texas, I started working for a small company that financed and operated large energy projects. After much effort we were only able to secure one customer after three years. Needless to say, this was not enough to keep us all employed. One day

Driven To Our Knees

we were called into the conference room and told that we were going to be let go. After the meeting I was pulled aside by the CEO and told that his brother had contacted one of his contractors and told them that I would be a good addition to their company. That was five years ago and I'm still employed with that company now.

The longest time I was without work was one week. I essentially had another job within 24 hours of being laid off, through no direct effort of my own. God had worked through other people to provide for my family and me.

God works behind the scenes in our behalf. He works through people whom we don't know to bless us. He will put us in the right place at the right time, to talk to someone in the right way, about the right thing. He controls all the variables – without my knowledge or intervention. He blesses me in ways I could not have imagined. Why – to show that He is God; that He is good. My current job is the fruit of His goodness.

Key Point: The fruit of God's goodness are His miracles.

Key Point: Nothing is impossible with God. He doesn't need our help.

How has God helped you, in an unexpected way?

He Saved Me From Myself

How many times have you made a bad decision that you wish you could reverse? We all can say "too many times". Even though you may have had to suffer the consequences, God saw you through it. He may have even fixed the mess you started.

God doesn't "reverse" all of our bad decisions, but saves us from enough of them to show us another aspect of His character – His mercy. Sometimes I don't need a reckless driver causing havoc in my life; I can do it all by myself. But when I get on my knees and seek the Lord with all my heart, He chooses to show me mercy; He doesn't leave me or says to me, "Fool, look what you've done!" He shows me mercy. He picks me up and allows me to get back in fellowship with Him. He even says in His word that if any man needs wisdom, let him ask (James 1:5 – 8). He does this because He is good in nature.

Key Point: The fruit of God's goodness is His mercy.

Driven To Our Knees

Summary

The most effective way to learn the goodness of God is to look at your own life, honestly. If we take time to reflect, we'll see how a powerful, righteous and holy God, has shown us mercy, grace, protection, comfort, peace, joy, prosperity, and love. These "fruits" are not produced based on our efforts, but are the product of a God whose character is only good.

The "good" that I enjoy in life (towb), is the result of God's good character (agathos).

Footnote:

As I reviewed this lesson, I re-read the 23rd Psalm. This lesson focuses on verse 4, but the whole Psalm is rich with the fruit of God's "agathos". What are the fruit (towb) of His goodness:

- He is a shepherd – a protector
- We will not be in want – He supplies or needs
- He gives us peace and restores us
- He guides us
- He is present with us
- He comforts us
- He will bless abundantly in the midst of our enemies
- He gives us His Spirit which purifies us and makes us Holy
- He provides good things to us
- He loves us every day of our lives
- He allows us to dwell with Him forever

God is truly Good.

Driven To Our Knees

Notes:

Complete Surrender: The Key to Victory

Introduction

In the *Prepared for Service* Bible study I spoke of a trial I was experiencing that seemed to last a long time. At first I would try to fix things myself and after that didn't work, I would pray and ask the Lord for help. After struggling a while, I exhausted all my options. Seemingly I had my "back against the wall" with no way out. If I was going to survive, the Lord would have to intervene. I had finally "surrendered", i.e., I had truly left the consequences up to the Lord to do whatever He saw was best. In actuality, this was the first step to my victory.

In the natural world, victory and surrender are mutually exclusive; there is no way to have a victory by surrendering. But in the life of a Christian, the key to victory over every trial we may experience is in our complete surrender of the situation to Christ. This Bible study discusses how the road to victory goes through the valley of surrender.

Scriptures Used In This Lesson
Matthew 26:36 – 46
Mark 14:32 – 42
Luke 22:40 – 46
Psalm 37:4
Deuteronomy 4:29 – 31
Deuteronomy 8:17 – 18

"…Not My Will…"

The most important example of complete surrender occurred in the garden of Gethsemane. The Bible highlights this example in Matthew 26, Mark 14, and Luke 22. After the Last Supper, Jesus went to the garden to pray. It was the night before his crucifixion. In Matthew 26:37, we learn that Jesus began to be "sorrowful and troubled" (NIV).

In Luke 22:44, the Bible says that Jesus was in "an agony" (KJV). The Greek for agony is "agonia" which means: of severe mental struggles and emotions, agony, anguish. Jesus was so stressed that His sweat was "great drops of blood falling down to the ground" (KJV). This physical condition doesn't happen very often, but in times of severe stress, capillaries that carry blood near the surface of the skin can rupture and blood can come out of the sweat glands.

I used to wonder, "Why was He stressed out? He knew everything; He knew that God would bring Him back to life. Why would He worry so much?" I thought about it a lot. We are not told exactly

Driven To Our Knees

what was going through His mind, but one possible reason occurred to me. Jesus had experienced oneness with God for all eternity. He had experienced the closeness, complete joy, peace and love of the Father in the most intimate way, for an infinite number of years before. Now all of a sudden, He would be separated from the Father...completely...for our sins.

The pain and humiliation of crucifixion at the hand of ungodly men was bad enough, but to willingly be totally separated from God, to experience "complete" death, I think, was almost unbearable for Jesus. He had to experience *two* deaths, one due to crucifixion and the other due to taking on the sins of the billions of people who have ever, and will ever live. To do this willingly was "complete" surrender.

Key Point: The greatest act of love ever given to you was Christ willingly giving His life for you.

Three times Jesus prayed that the "cup" of death be taken away from Him, but acknowledged that the will of the Father would prevail ("...yet not as I will, but as you will.",Matthew 26:39, NIV).

So Jesus, twice drinking from the "cup of death", is the greatest example of "complete surrender". Now how does this apply to us?

Surrender – What Does It Mean?
First, let's define surrender. According to the dictionary, to surrender means:

> **1 a :** to yield to the power, control, or possession of another upon compulsion or demand <*surrendered* the fort> **b :** to give up completely or agree to forgo especially in favor of another
> **2 a :** to give (oneself) up into the power of another especially as a prisoner **b :** to give (oneself) over to something (as an influence)
> *intransitive senses* : to give oneself up into the power of another : **YIELD**

This definition completely fits how our relationship should be with our Heavenly Father. If God loves us unconditionally, and only wants the very best for us, and wants to bless us, and knows every detail of our future, and is all powerful, and is sovereign, and is merciful, and is full of grace, why wouldn't we surrender to Him? If we want the best for our lives, it just makes sense to surrender to Him. So surrendering to Him opens the door for Him to work on our behalf, according to His timetable, and His divine purpose for our lives.

Most of the time, we don't surrender because of our desire for "self-control" or pride. Our desire to do things our way overrides the "common sense" approach of surrendering to God. Surrendering to God is really contrary to our fallen nature. That's why we need to have a "new nature", i.e., be "born again" in order to surrender. So how do we surrender?

How Do I Surrender?

First, you have to acknowledge and confess your sins. This means realizing that you have had thoughts, attitudes and actions that have separated you from God. You need to acknowledge that you can't get close to God without help and that you need someone to "bridge the gap" between you and God. If you are not saved, you need to ask Christ to come into your life. If you are saved, you need to ask the Father to help you become more sensitive and obedient to the Holy Spirit, Who dwells in you. But this assumes that you have a desire to change. You have to see the need and want to change.

The second step in the process of surrendering involves experiencing trials and tribulations. This may sound odd, but trials and tribulations can produce more "fruit" in our lives than good times…if we respond properly. We experience several stages when we go through a trial:

1. Initial shock and pain
2. We work to get out of it
3. Pray and ask God to help us get out of it
4. Work some more to get out of it on our own
5. Give up and let God work things out on our behalf

It's the last stage that produces the fruit. When we "give up" (surrender), God begins to work in us, our circumstances, and other people to bring about His purpose. Only He can produce good out of a tragedy. Ultimately, He will be glorified, i.e., He will receive credit for the good and benefits that come from the trial.

Most of the time we have a tendency to reach step #5 only after we are exhausted and beat up emotionally, physically and spiritually. We will try every other option before we truly give up to God. There is an unbiblical quote that drives a lot of our thinking:

"God helps them that help themselves."

The truth is that God helps those to seek Him with their whole hearts. Read Deuteronomy 4:29 – 31. When we are in distress, we tend to turn to God. Our relationship with Him is strengthened. He encourages us to stay close to Him by working in our behalf; doing things that we never thought of, through people we never thought of, sometimes people we've never known. We are amazed at how

Driven To Our Knees

He works. Another occasion has presented itself for us to get close to Him. This is step #5. We must surrender in order to receive the fruit of knowing Him.

Key Point: "God does His best work without our help": *Pastor Carl A. Lucas, Sr., 5/22/05*

So when a trial comes, realize that it is coming through the almighty hand of God and we need to move quickly to step #5. The sooner we move to that stage and God accomplishes His purpose, the quicker the trial will come to an end.

Can you think of a situation that initially appeared to be "bad" but ultimately produced a good result? Can you see that type of situation developing in your life now?

Why do we have such a hard time moving to step #5? How can we get there more quickly?

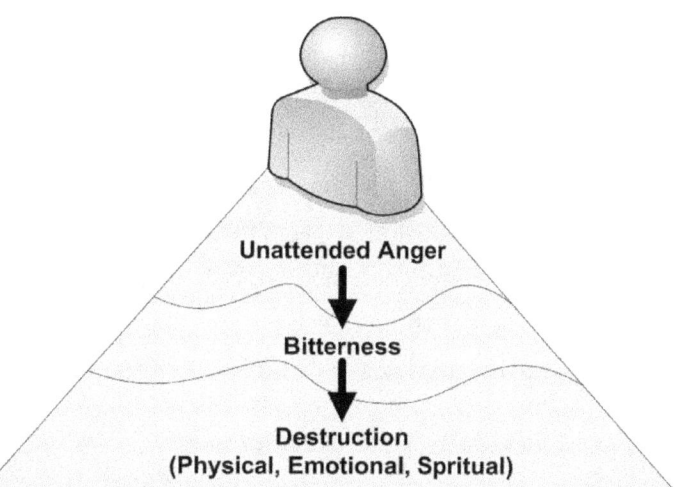

A third step to surrendering is forgiveness. Everybody has been wronged in their lives...sometimes to the extent of extreme pain and suffering. It's only natural to feel anger, outrage, and sadness because of being wronged. But the long-term effects of these feelings will tend to separate us from God and damage other relationships in our lives. Unattended anger leads to bitterness; bitterness, left untouched, will grow like a weed and destroy every good thing around you, including yourself.

When we come to the Father and say, "Lord, these people have caused me so much pain and heartache...but I ask that you help me forgive..." then we begin the process that allows God to "make things right", and protect ourselves from further damage. To forgive means that you "give up" (surrender) your right of revenge; you surrender the right to have the offender(s) "pay you back". You say, in a sense, "Lord, You handle the situation; I just want to be in right relationship with you." You place your relationship with Him above your feelings.

Driven To Our Knees

Key Point: To forgive means that you choose to "give up" (surrender) your right of revenge; you surrender the right to have the offender(s) "pay you back". You first make a choice; your feelings will tend to "normalize" over time.

Forgiveness is not easy nor does it happen overnight. We need to recognize that it is a process that begins with a choice, not a feeling.

Can you think of someone who let anger turn to bitterness? How did it affect their lives and the lives of others around them? What was the end result of their bitterness?

The fourth step in surrendering involves giving up our desires, and choosing for His will to be done in our lives. This is very difficult for us because it goes against our nature. But if we surrender our will, God will bless us in ways we can't imagine.

One of my favorite Psalms is Psalm 37. One of the more popular verses is verse 4.

Delight yourself in the LORD and he will give you the desires of your heart. (NIV)

On the surface we think, "All I have to do is to be happy about God and I can get what I want". But there's more to it than that. "Delighting" ourselves in the Lord involves molding our will to His; thinking along the same lines as God; truly being delighted to be in His presence, being delighted to pray to Him; being delighted to know Him. The focus of the verse is Him, not our wants and desires. And notice who will provide the desires of our hearts…God, not us. If we truly "delight" ourselves in God and make Him the focal point of our lives, then our desires will be more in line with His desires for us. Then, He will supply what is best, at the right time, in the right way, in the right amount.

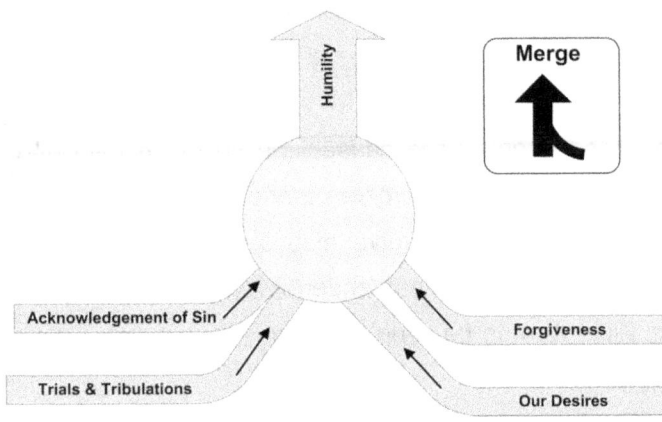

The Roads To Surrender

Once we understand the benefits of putting God first, it doesn't make sense to get our needs and desires met any other way.

When we look at the four ways to surrender, all roads lead to humility before God. Humility is the opposite of pride. Humility opens the door for God to move in our lives and for us to

Driven To Our Knees

get close to Him. As we get closer two things increase in our lives — our obedience to Him and our faith (trust) in Him.

When we are humble, we step out of God's way. We must always remember who is the source of our help, wealth, and wellbeing. Read Deuteronomy 8:17 – 18. It is God who is the source of all things good in our lives. So why not allow Him to work in our behalf?

Summary

When we are going through trials, the key to victory is to get to step #5 as quickly as possible. Surrender to the Lord; it is the most reasonable thing to do. The quicker we become humble before Him, i.e., surrender, the more quickly we will see Him work in our lives and receive glory.

Driven To Our Knees

Notes:

Answers To Prayers

The purpose of this section is to assist in developing the realization that God "does" answer prayer. When documenting your requests, keep these things in mind:

- Is this request consistent with God's plan/purpose for my life?
- Can God be glorified through this request?
- Is this a need or desire?
- God will not grant a request that violates His word or principles.

Date: _____

Request: _____

_____

_____

Answer to Request: _____

_____

_____

Date: _____

Request: _____

_____

_____

Answer to Request: _____

_____

_____

Date: _____

Request: _____

_____

_____

Answer to Request: _____

_____

_____

Date: _____

Request: _____

_____

_____

Answer to Request: _____

_____

_____

═══

Date: _____

Request: _____

_____

_____

Answer to Request: _____

_____

_____

═══

Date: _____

Request: _____

_____

_____

Answer to Request: _____

_____

_____

===

Date: _____

Request: _____

_____

_____

Answer to Request: _____

_____

_____

Your Blessing Book

In this section, document the ways the Lord has blessed you. Over time, you will be encouraged as you read all that He has done in your life. Try this every day for thirty days. Please feel free to copy this page as many times as you need. Use the Notes section to and any thoughts or related scriptures.

Date: _____

Blessing: _____

_____

_____

_____

==

Date: _____

Blessing: _____

_____

_____

_____

==

Date: _____

Blessing: _____

_____

_____

_____

==

Date: _____

Blessing: _____

_____

_____

_____

═══

Date: _____

Blessing: _____

_____

_____

_____

═══

Date: _____

Blessing: _____

_____

_____

_____

═══

Notes: _____

_____

_____

Date: _____

Blessing: _____

_____

_____

_____

Date: _____

Blessing: _____

_____

_____

_____

Date: _____

Blessing: _____

_____

_____

_____

Notes: _____

_____

_____

Date: _____

Blessing: _____

_____

_____

_____

===

Date: _____

Blessing: _____

_____

_____

_____

===

Date: _____

Blessing: _____

_____

_____

_____

===

Notes: _____

_____

_____

Date: _____

Blessing: _____

_____

_____

_____

===

Date: _____

Blessing: _____

_____

_____

_____

===

Date: _____

Blessing: _____

_____

_____

_____

===

Notes: _____

_____

_____

Date: _____

Blessing: _____

_____

_____

_____

===

Date: _____

Blessing: _____

_____

_____

_____

===

Date: _____

Blessing: _____

_____

_____

_____

===

Notes: _____

_____

_____

Date: _____

Blessing: _____

_____

_____

_____

═══

Date: _____

Blessing: _____

_____

_____

_____

═══

Date: _____

Blessing: _____

_____

_____

_____

═══

Notes: _____

_____

_____

Date: _____

Blessing: _____

_____

_____

_____

===

Date: _____

Blessing: _____

_____

_____

_____

===

Date: _____

Blessing: _____

_____

_____

_____

===

Notes: _____

_____

_____

Date: _____

Blessing: _____

_____

_____

_____

═══

Date: _____

Blessing: _____

_____

_____

_____

═══

Date: _____

Blessing: _____

_____

_____

_____

═══

Notes: _____

_____

_____

Date: _____

Blessing: _____

_____

_____

_____

===

Date: _____

Blessing: _____

_____

_____

_____

===

Date: _____

Blessing: _____

_____

_____

_____

===

Notes: _____

_____

_____

(This page is intentionally blank)

(This page is intentionally blank)

(This page is intentionally blank)

(This page is intentionally blank)

www.ingramcontent.com/pod-product-compliance
Lightning Source LLC
Chambersburg PA
CBHW081458040426
42446CB00016B/3301